MW01032354

Dear Professor Huntington,
Thank you for all you do
for LAS!

Zizi

After Democracy

After Democracy

Imagining Our Political Future

Zizi Papacharissi

Yale UNIVERSITY PRESS

New Haven & London

Yale University Press

New Haven & London

Copyright © 2021 by Zizi Papacharissi.

All rights reserved.

This book may not be reproduced, in whole or in part, including illustrations, in any form (beyond that copying permitted by Sections 107 and 108 of the U.S. Copyright Law and except by reviewers for the public press), without written permission from the publishers.

Yale University Press books may be purchased in quantity for educational, business, or promotional use. For information, please e-mail sales.press@yale.edu (U.S. office) or sales@yaleup.co.uk (U.K. office).

Set in Janson type by IDS Infotech Ltd.
Printed in the United States of America.

ISBN 978-0-300-24596-7 (alk. paper)
Library of Congress Control Number: 2020939832
A catalogue record for this book is available from the British Library.

This paper meets the requirements of ANSI/NISO Z39.48-1992
(Permanence of Paper).

10 9 8 7 6 5 4 3 2 1

To strangers and citizens of the world,
my conversational companions

Contents

Contents

Preface

Think. Upside down. High and low brow.
Forget what you know.
Rethink what you believe.
Listen, to learn.
Reimagine.

Democracy has long been considered an ideal state of governance. What if it's not? Perhaps it is not the end goal but, rather, the transition stage to something better. We have lent our cheer and support and sacrificed lives for revolutions meant to place democracy where it does not exist. But change is gradual. Revolutions are long. They have to be long, so as to attain meaning. And revolutions, noble as they may be, often lead away from and not toward democracy. What if democracy is not an ideal state or an end goal? What if there is something better out there, and technology can help us uncover a long-hidden path to it?

We have been through many iterations of democracy. Through each one, we thought we had it right. When we privileged property owners with the right to vote, when we excluded women from the voting process, and when we kept people from voting because of the color of their skin, we naively claimed what we had was a democracy. We have made much progress in advancing equality in our governance systems, but we have not reached perfection and perhaps never will. Bear in mind that in our collective past, we have called many governments democratic that, in retrospect, were not. Democracy has always felt within reach and yet forever out of sight.

Democracy is not the final stop on our civic journey. Technology can push us further. This is the premise of this book: to think about and beyond democracy, to imagine a different role in all of this for technology.

There are many ways to go about this. My goal was to trace desire lines that would organically take us to what might follow democracy. So I decided to travel the world and strike up conversations with strangers. I am a social scientist who has been studying democracy and technology for more than two decades. Using a variety of research methods, I have listened, learned, and communicated my findings on how technology can help us tell stories that unite us, identify us, or potentially further divide us. For this project, I was asking people to imagine something that does not exist. People were to think about a future state of democracy and how to get there through technology. These are not things that we think about every day, and these are not questions that can be easily answered when posed out of the blue. So I thought that if I engaged people in casual conversation about democracy, citizenship, and what the future might hold, I might be able to better jump-start this process. So I mapped out an ambitious plan that included one hundred countries that I wanted to visit. I wrote up my intentions and obtained approval for my process from our institutional review board at the University of Illinois at Chicago. As I was setting up my travel plans, one of the reviewers for this book called my plan bold but also too broad and advised me to work with a more targeted group of countries. So I chose from a group of options to include countries that had seen tumultuous and calm times, that were sometimes characterized as democracies and sometimes not, and that presented places where democracy had triumphed but had also failed. It was not to be the traveling marathon that I envisioned, but it gave me representation and took me down an interesting path. I will tell you which countries these were in chapter 1.

Have you ever found yourself engrossed in a conversation about civics with a cab driver? Shared a couple of words of civic wisdom that left you utterly fulfilled with the person who checked you out at the grocery store? Engaged in random politics banter with a fellow passenger on a train or a plane? That was the set of circumstances I was seeking to re-create as I approached or was introduced to strangers around the world. Typically, following a casual conversation, they would ask me what I do, and I would say that I study social media and politics. This never fails to spark follow-up questions, so I would explain what I was working on. I worked with friends and colleagues, used my networks, and asked all, including those I had already interviewed, to introduce me to other folks who might be interested in chatting with me. I looked at places where I would encounter people different from me, so I worked outside academia. I learned to glean political ideology through the initial conversation so that I could diversify my sample. I moved in circles different from those my everyday routines would take me into and approached people, established connections, and asked for introductions to others. It was a randomized yet strategic path, designed to take me out of the familiar. Once my conversational companions gave me permission to interview them, I asked them all the same three questions and never deviated from my pattern. The questions were, What is democracy? What is citizenship? What might make democracy better?

I ran one hundred interviews. Sometimes I asked people who looked different from me to run them, and I trained them for it, so as to avoid bias. My friends, colleagues, and students helped.

I speak German, Greek, and some Spanish, so I conducted most interviews on my own and used translators on a few occasions. As I wrapped up my interviews, I asked my conversational companions how they wanted to be identified. Some chose a name, which I noted. Most insisted on using their own name. A few wanted to be anonymous. As I debriefed them and shared my contact information so that we could stay in touch and so that I might share the book with them, they all, without fail, asked, "What did other people say? Similar or different things from what I said?" "They said the same things," I would respond, "but they used different words." All were surprised. I interviewed people in refugee centers, and my respondents from Libya, Afghanistan, Pakistan, Syria, and Egypt, to name a few, were intrigued that their responses on the meaning of democracy and citizenship were so close to responses that people in the United Kingdom, Germany, and the United States provided. My conversational companions in the United Kingdom, Canada, Greece, Mexico, and Brazil, to name a few more, were struck that their responses were conceptually close to what those I interviewed in China and Russia told me. So was I.

I thought I might find traces of a great global disconnect when it comes to how we think about democracy and citizenship. I figured that for sure there would be grand differences across countries in what people thought was wrong with democracy. I was hoping to use their thoughts on what was wrong to map out what "right" might look like. The goal was, after all, to sketch out what we aspire toward, what we think of when we imagine an ideal democracy, or if it's not a democracy, what might lie after it. There is no massive disconnect. We may, in fact, want to think about whether the impression that there is a disconnect could be a manufactured one.

Sure, people use different words to communicate their thoughts, in different languages, and language conveys nuance. For example, the German word for citizenship is *Staatsbürgerschaft* or *Staatsange-hörigkeit*. Both words are created by combining *Staat*, which means "state or country," and *bürgerschaft* (citizenship) or *angehörigkeit* (affiliation). So, for example, when I asked what citizenship means in German, I received responses that began with being affiliated with or a resident of Germany. Still, as the conversation progressed into topics that characterize citizenship, almost all responses coalesced around common themes.

What were common strands that emerged as people talked with me about the first question: What is democracy? You can read about these in chapter 2. There was more agreement than disagreement as people first went silent and fell into long pauses. They were both at a want and at a loss for words when confronted with this question. Silence was the first theme that I encountered in response to this question. It was followed by leaning into familiar definitions of democracy and expressing ambivalence about them. Familiarity and ambivalence meant that people expressed a clear understanding of what form democracy is supposed to take and an astute sense that it does not exist in that form. Equality was the third common theme when defining democracy, although most were quick to point out that equality is a complex concept and that it may be based on but definitely moves beyond the right to vote. Then naturally conversations drifted to the fourth theme that emerged, voice, followed by the fifth theme, skepticism about the ability to achieve voice and equality in contemporary democracies. So a conversational trope that moved from silence to familiarity and ambivalence to equality, voice, and skepticism emerged as people sought to define democracy.

I then asked what citizenship meant to people and found two prominent themes, nobility and invisibility. You can read more about the civic dreams and letdowns of my conversational companions in chapter 3. Suffice it to say that they spoke with me about their deepest desires to contribute to democracy with words that were noble, earnest, and dedicated. They then observed how often, despite their best efforts, they felt overlooked, disregarded, and ignored. These conversations gave me some ideas about how technology might mend these concerns, although, strikingly, technology was rarely brought up by my conversational companions. When they spoke about misinformation or propaganda spread through media, most attributed that to specific stakeholders, corporations, and politicians, and not the media per se.

In the end, we talked about what might make democracy better. My conversational companions knew what I was after. I had explained that I was writing a book about democracy and what might make it better, so they were primed to imagine that future with me. Most said that democracy can be made better by fixing what is wrong with it: populism, corruption, and a general lack of educated leaders. These are the core themes, recounted in chapter 4. They sound obvious enough, but the poignancy, insight, and clarity with which they were communicated to me are worth reading about.

So then I started picking up traces of conversations in which people made very specific suggestions about what we might improve and mapping how those overlapped. I further noted instances when they had told me they felt democracy was really working, examples of times when they felt civically fulfilled. I also thought about the problems they had brought up and what it might take to fix them. I read up on possible solutions and spent time mulling those over myself. In the end, I came up with ten paths forward: these included advocating for *soft capitalism* and stronger democracy, implementing more forms of *micro-governance*, finding ways to *count absence* from civic processes, outlining *long- and short-term political goals* for governments, introducing modes of civic engagement in addition to and *beyond voting*, requiring *civic education for all* politicians, designing media that do not elevate populism and training ourselves to *forget messiahs*, learning to *game the system* so as to move news media and headlines beyond the economics of attention, *reinventing journalism* as a civic conduit, and finally, *being our own civic agents of change*.

I see these as solutions working together and being effective only if implemented concurrently. The process of change will be gradual and slow and may lead us to missteps that will sometimes be painful. Let's look at this as growing pains, because we are advancing to the next stage, which will be a form of transhuman democracy. Technology will be even more ubiquitous, in ways that permeate every fiber of our civic being. Our capabilities will be further augmented by technologies, and our lifestyles will continue to evolve into routines that blur boundaries, which creates a security of the familiar for us. All of the platforms we use today will be irrelevant in a few years, replaced by technology so ingrained in our every day that it will be unnoticeable. We will become transhuman, and this should not scare us, as long as we define what transhuman will mean. That is as far as I can take this prediction. I completed this work as the Covid-19 pandemic was beginning to emerge in some parts of the world. The conditions being confronted around the world during the pandemic further reinforce my conclusions. We do not possess a way of predicting our future. Still, voice, fairness, literacy, and education matter. We must acknowledge our faults in order to change. And change is often the only option we have to survive. We have no way of knowing what will follow. The future is uncertain, and there is no escaping the desire lines of democracy—past, present, and future. All we know is that to be democratic, we must be human first. And to be transhuman, we must allow ourselves the opportunity to change. We have to permit democracy to evolve alongside us.

We change and so does our technology, but we cling to past iterations of democracy like a dream we desperately try to remember after we wake up. We believe that by staying true to long-gone versions of democracy, we will restore its authenticity. We see observing civic rituals of the past as a way of resolving the problems of the present. But we need to create a democracy that is designed for our time, with built-in flexibility to adjust to our future. Yet we use democratic models that do not fit our times, and it feels like struggling to get into the outfits we wore as teenagers sometimes. Let's be adults. Civic adults. Find a democracy that fits us. Life is never static. Neither is democracy.

Acknowledgments

Inspiration for this book emerged as I traveled and gave invited talks, keynotes, and plenaries on my work on technology and politics. As I chatted with my hosts, strolled around with traveling companions, or just caught up with friends, conversation always returned to the topic of democracy. So I have to thank my friends, my acquaintances, and the accidental strangers who contributed their time and thoughts in conversing with me so generously. They inspired me to embark on a journey around the world to speak with strangers about democracy.

I then have to thank my conversational companions all over the globe. I found you in refugee centers, taxicabs, parks, and cafés; spaces public, private, or a little bit of both. You were earnest, thoughtful, and forthcoming with your time. I appreciate your dedication. I am grateful, honored, and humbled by your honesty and insightfulness. A book can only be as strong as the ideas that it rests on. I am thankful for the unique, original, and deeply personal views you shared with me. I appreciate your openness and imagination.

I am further indebted to friends, colleagues, and acquaintances who helped me expand my global network of connections and thus grow my intercontinental salon of conversational companions. I particularly want to thank my childhood friend Olga, who was instrumental in connecting me with the refugee networks I became involved with. Maria de Fatima Oliveira helped me run interviews in Brazil and has always been an enthusiastic supporter of my work. I thank her for her kind heart, and I appreciate her smarts deeply. I further want to thank Chad Van De Wiele and Jamie Foster Campbell for helping me complete interviews in the United States and Canada. My gratitude goes to Paige Gibson, who helped me complete interviews that balanced my sample from Germany. Funding for my research came from a University Scholar grant, awarded by the University of Illinois. I am grateful to the University of Illinois system and my home campus of Chicago, in particular, for their consistent support and encouragement.

Above all, I want to thank my students, because they are constant sources of inspiration. One of the places where I feel most alive is the classroom, a place that I enter to teach but one where I find myself constantly learning, stretching my imagination, and rethinking who I am.

Finally, I want to thank my mother, Stella, for raising me to be an independent thinker, a strong woman, a self-reliant human, a good listener, and above all for encouraging me to be different. As a child, I remember once requesting a pair of sneakers because everybody else at school had them. "Why on earth would you want to be like everybody else?" she responded. This book is about not being like everybody else. It is about listening to people's stories to understand what makes them different yet still somehow connects them to each other.

After Democracy

ONE

What If?

It is fall, and I am in Mexico City. It is warm and breezy but grows hotter as my cab gets caught in early morning traffic. The driver rolls the window down, lets out a long sigh, and apologizes for the inconvenience. It's okay, I explain. I grew up in Greece and now live in Chicago. I travel a lot. I understand traffic. I am in no rush. A casual conversation evolves in Spanish and English, and my driver, Louis, connects traffic to many of Mexico's contemporary problems. Corruption, he says, is the biggest. "This is not democracy," he says at a red light. He explains that only a few people have access to power or can run for office. "These people feel more like kings. The faces are new, but the habits are old."

It is winter, and I am in Beijing. I walk in the Temple of the Sun Gardens with Gary, a tour guide originally from the Szechwan province. He points out trees to my right and explains that they are five hundred years old. People gather around the benches, pedestrian bridges, and long corridors that lead through the garden to the temple. They are caught up in card games, some with dramatic climaxes, all in the backdrop of casual conversation. They are mostly retirees, Gary explains. They enjoy gathering in the gardens, despite the bitter cold. Gary is a bright, quick-witted guy who tells me stories about the gardens, the city, his life. Though he is typically fast with a quip in response to most of my questions, he pauses when I ask him to explain democracy. He stays silent for some time. "Hard to say," he finally responds.

It is spring, but it does not feel like it. I am in St. Petersburg, Russia. Chunks of ice travel down the Neva River, as the city begins to respond to the rays of sunlight that sneak in through my car window. It's bitter cold, but the sun shines brightly. "Sun with teeth" is what we call this in Greece, I tell Valeria, my traveling companion. She is a photojournalist from Belarus. She spent the past few hours taking pictures up and down Nevsky Prospect. "Here's an abandoned guitar on the pavement," she says as she points to a photo on her camera. She points to another photo of the guitar being carried by a man, who picked up the instrument after she photographed it. "Was it his?" I ask. "No," she responds. "I think he thought it was valuable because I took a photo of it." She talks more about wandering through neighborhoods and documenting the habits and small dramas of everyday life. As a journalist, she spends time interviewing locals in disadvantaged neighborhoods. She describes how citizens attempt to take care of their community. "I realized these people had simple dreams, all about doing the day's work perfectly," she says. I am reminded of what Richard Sennett wrote in *The Craftsman*: doing one thing and doing it well for its own sake.[1] As I am silently pondering this, it feels like Valeria has been reading my mind. "For me," she says, "this is a good citizen."

It is still spring, but it feels more like summer. I am in Thessaloniki, in Greece, and walking along the promenade with Cristina. We stop to look at some skaters and BMX bikers, who are using the space around a statue of Alexander the Great as a ramp to perform stunts. Like the country itself, it is a mesmerizing collapse of the past into the present. Cristina is head of exports at a local food company. She grew up in Quito, Ecuador, and spent time studying in Washington, D.C., and Italy, before moving to Greece. "Democracy is whatever you want it to be," she says. "It is how we put it to work that restricts or empowers us."

It is true. We have considered democracy as our primary mode of governance for hundreds and hundreds of years. We have supported revolutions to help put it in place. We have resisted regimes that threaten to overthrow it. We have been disappointed when revolutions also led away from democracy, instead of toward it. As shown in the preceding vignettes, I ask people what democracy is and am met with complaints and nostalgia but never a specific definition. As societies, we have called many forms of government "democracy." When we privileged property owners, men, or whites with the right to vote, we still claimed democracy. We have made much progress in advancing equality in our governance systems, but we are far from perfection. Can technology bring us closer to governance by popular will? Will it push us further away?

Democracy is better suited for smaller societies, where it originated. The city-state republics of ancient Greece, along with independent republic formations that emerged in India at around the same time, served to organize the deliberative governance needs of fewer citizens. Because only male property owners were afforded civic rights, they often resembled deliberative governance systems run by the aristocracy. Still, they established the mythos of deliberative assemblies that decide on governance. This form of direct deliberation as governance established a premise. Contemporary citizens of large-scale democracies long for direct contact with their governments. The absence of direct contact has led to cynicism against media that fail to connect citizens to politicians and against politicians who are unavailable to the masses. Failures in representation, tied to times of financial insecurity, have encouraged waves of populism at present but also throughout history. Democracy is hard. Populism promises easy solutions premised on a false sense of closeness, intimacy. Citizens want to hear that they are understood. They want to be told that they matter, face-to-face. And they want solutions. Direct democracy provides these things. Representative democracy complicates them. Capitalism exploits these wants. Populism makes empty promises. And thus, the cycle of hope and disillusionment continues.

Technologies further lend fodder to our hopes and fears about democracy. Facebook and Twitter augmented the voices and hopes of several mass social movements, including those referred to as the Arab Spring. Loud as those digitally amplified voices became, they were not able to produce harmony across the region. The unfinished revolutions of the Arab Spring illustrate how technology can invite both optimism and apprehension. What is the meaning of technology for politics, for democracy? My most recent work has focused on tracking sentiment expression online, through big and deep data analysis.[2] With my colleagues, we have examined prominent movements and their online presence, including several Arab Spring movements, #Occupy, #BlackLivesMatter, #daca, and #maga. We tracked their activity online through monitoring and analyzing the social media feeds developed around these hashtags. No matter the context, I always return to the same conclusion.

Technology does not rectify the democratic condition. It does not provide easy fixes to complex problems, and it often cultivates powerful misconceptions. The internet is not a magic wand, and neither were the technologies that preceded it. Net-based platforms cannot render democracy where it did not exist in the first place. Platforms like Facebook and Twitter offer *public space* for conversation but do not render a robust *public sphere*. They connect people and offer them opportunities to express themselves. Yet they offer no guarantee that this communication will produce consensus. Like all public spaces, they connect us with new people, but they also render us vulnerable to attacks from strangers, as we've seen with the presidential election of 2016 in the United States, the Brexit referendum in 2016, the election in France in 2017, and the general elections in Brazil and Mexico in 2018, to name a few. Further, social media *pluralize* expression and connection, but they do not necessarily *democratize*. They open more paths to connection, but those connections do not necessarily lead to democratization. They connect underrepresented and marginalized people; they also connect fascists. Finally, social media *amplify* but they do not *equalize*. Technology augments voice but not on equal terms for all, and it does not possess the power to extinguish social problems. The internet does not create hate speech, for instance; people do. Still, social media platforms make acts of hate more visible and thus more easily spreadable. The architecture of platforms reinforces and reproduces existing hierarchies of power, through cultural biases that permeate both its design and how it is put to use.

Keeping all of this in mind, is there a better way?

To be clear, I refer to representative forms of governance and not monarchies, oligarchies, dictatorships, and various other authoritarian models. To consider our options, we need to see the shortfalls of contemporary democracies. Addressing these shortfalls and practicing their solutions would help us approach a better state of democratic governance. This would be a modality of governance that anticipates the conflicts presented by capitalism and contains mechanisms that permit us to enhance equality in representation and governance. It might be an iteration of democracy that connects citizens to media and politicians through paths, digital and non-digital, that permit healthier relationships of trust to emerge. I'm not trapped in some utopian vision: I believe citizens have the answers to these problems, but they are rarely asked to provide them and almost never listened to. This book offers citizens' voices.

As discussed, people without property, those who were not men, and people of color have all been excluded in "democratic" systems. Several conditions are no doubt missing from the democratic equation at present without us fully realizing what they are yet. The problems we presently experience with misinformation and disinformation suggest abuses of power connected to a lack of information literacy. The inability to address these issues prompts us to think about whether our elected officials really understand these problems and can fix them. Corruption influences how governments run democracies. Recent social movements point to a lack of representative equality that misrepresents the public's interests.

Conversations with citizens of the world can help us think through the past, present, and future of democracy. Weaving the stories of citizens of the world together can lead to a more compelling narrative about democracy. And perhaps technology, sometimes an ally and frequently a foe of democracy, can be put to wiser use. What if there is something better and technology can help us reach it, rather than move away from it?

It is this process that led me to the present work. What better way to find out, I thought, than to ask people directly for their thoughts about democracy. Not in the context of focused and structured interviews, but in the relaxed atmosphere of a café, in the confined space of a cab ride in the busy streets of an uber-modern city, during a stroll down paths that overlap rural and urban sceneries, or in the harsh realities presented by the dwellings of a refugee camp. So I set out to travel the world and strike up conversations with random strangers from the many walks of life that connect, identify, and potentially disconnect us. I chatted with folks on the realities of their everyday lives, and as we began to flow into the joyful rhythms of banter, I asked about democracy. I explained my project and asked whether they might be interested in sharing their insights. I ended up with one hundred conversations. I asked all of my companions in this random, impromptu yet organized interviews the same three questions:

What is democracy?
What does it mean to be a citizen?
What could make democracy better?

As I have argued elsewhere, technologies network us, *but it is our stories that connect us, identify us, or further divide us.*[3] Democracy and technology are about expression and connection. I would like to listen to and share people's stories about democracy, use them to figure out the place of technology in democracy, and let these stories pave the way to what may follow and improve democracy. After democracy, what?

Learning from the Past

Bottom-up as I aspired for the research in this book to be, my work still draws from theory and hopes to generate theory, in the form of distilled recommendations and a refined understanding of what might follow democracy. As an idealized form of governance, democracy has always harbored our adoration and discontent. Recent waves of civil unrest throughout the Middle East and North Africa mobilized the masses with the promise of democratic governance, only to result in a mess of conflicted and unsettled geopolitical interests and many human casualties. Revolutions of the past that inspire present movements were hardly the seamless processes of democratic transition that we prefer to remember. The French and American Revolutions overthrew monarchical states of exploitation, but the progress to democracy was long and filled with war, loss, uncertainty, and long interim periods in which powerful, semi-monarchical figures led the countries to more stable modes of representative democratic governance. Going back further, ancient Greece was marked by long periods of war and short intervals of peace between democratic and oligarchic city-states.

We forget our complex history with democracy in the haze of our collective nostalgia. We expect a lot from democracy, and when we do not receive it, we blame our politicians, the media, stakeholders, and capitalist interests—and for good reason. But it is not just our elected officials, media, and other mechanisms of governance that have let us down; it is our own expectations. We set impossible goals and unrealistic timelines. We are romanced by a fairy tale. Yet the truth is, we have always lived in imperfect democracies, and we still do.

Democracy is not static. It is not a given, it is not guaranteed, and it is not stable. *It is a state, not stasis.* And it is an imperfect state at that, often leaving citizens in the most advanced democracies unfulfilled or feeling uncounted.[4] Although this state is not new, it is amplified in the present era, in the sense that we feel that citizens of the past enjoyed something that we have lost, possibly forever. The past was better. The present is mediocre. The future is uncertain.

Thinking About the Present

The condition of democracy has driven much of my work. The democratic paradox, as the political theorist Chantal Mouffe refers to it, is the impossibility of practicing direct democracy in mass societies.[5] A democratic model created for small societies is now presented as the be-all and end-all for the problems of mass societies. In my first book, *A Private Sphere: Democracy in a Digital Age*, I questioned the relevance of conventional models of deliberation, including the public sphere, to the contemporary age.[6] The public sphere generally refers to open deliberation that can lead toward consensus in democratic decision-making. Jürgen Habermas's original and seminal text, however, used the word *öffentilichkeit*, chronically mistranslated as the "public sphere." His term refers to the potentiality of general openness in conversation and a society's ability to offer that. The term "public sphere," traced to its roots in ancient Greece, does not even translate properly in Greek, ancient or modern. The internet offers openness, I argued, but this imagined ideal of a public sphere is a metaphor meant to inspire, not actualize. I made the point that citizens in contemporary societies, disillusioned with conventional modes of political participation, seek to reinvent their own micro and macro political dreams and aspirations by availing themselves of newer media technologies. The public sphere leads directly to modes of expression that they are already cynical about, and the personal or domestic sphere is increasingly surveilled or monetized. Instead, citizens retreat to a mobile, largely psychic space termed the "private sphere," where they have the autonomy to practice politics in ways they deem meaningful.

How do they practice, and with what consequences? I traced those questions in my next book, *Affective Publics: Sentiment, Technology, and Politics*, by examining how people connect and mobilize around issues that concern them in contemporary societies. I defined "affective publics" as networked publics connected, reified, and, potentially, disbanded by sentiment. These feelings drive action that sometimes reflexively moves people forward but often also leaves them entrapped in a state of engaged passivity. In the end, I concluded, technologies network us, *but it is our stories that connect us, identify us, and potentially divide us.*

I did not realize it at the time, but inevitably I was leading myself to the questions I had been avoiding all along and that would form the basis of this work. What is it that people do with technologies? What is the consequence of this use for democracy? What does democracy become, and ultimately, what is democracy in contemporary societies? I had been motivated, of course, by the "what if" condition, the subjunctive mode, all along.[7] I knew what technologies did. But by asking what they were, I wanted to lure people into thinking along with me about what they could be instead. *What if* technology were put to a different use?

I had neglected, however, to apply the subjunctive mode to the main focus of my inquiry: democracy. Passionately as I had argued for reimagining our lives with technologies, I had forgotten to put democracy to the same test. So this is what this book is about: What if? Not just what if democracy were better, but what it would take to make it better. And, more important, what if democracy is not what we are after but the path to something else? What is that, and how do we find out? This presents the theoretical backdrop that inspires this work and the research that this work will engage and contribute to. That said, this book seeks to use theory to move beyond theory, to speak with citizens so as to speak directly to citizens.

A Plan for Reimagining the Future

When I first conceived of this project, I thought of it as an evolving travelogue.[8] There are 195 countries that make up our world, and I wanted to work from a reasonable sample, selected to reflect different approaches to democracy. I used the three questions on democracy, citizenship, and what might make democracy better as a guide in mapping the stories I heard. As I conducted initial interviews, I realized that there were meaningful ways in which I could organize my approach to be more faithful to my research objectives. I wanted to include but also move beyond Eurocentrism and theorizations of the West when it comes to democracy. I wanted to discuss the problems of our times—cynicism, disillusionment, populism— with people from around the world. These problems are not unique to our time. Still, they define our democracies. I decided to draw from a more focused list of countries that would allow me to tap into these problems, if I were to synthesize people's responses and evolve out of them. Therefore, I decided to focus on three varieties of regimes:

1. My first focus was democracies that are vibrant and have a long history but also are somehow flawed. These are democracies under distress. To obtain as broad a representation as possible, I worked with the following countries: Brazil, Canada, Greece, Mexico, the United Kingdom, and

the United States. I chose these because of their considerable experience with democracy but also because of their successes and recent difficulties with corruption, economic insecurity, and populism. The countries selected reflect a variety of ways in which democracies have responded to contemporary problems.

2. My second focus was regimes that are labeled as authoritarian by the West but are populated by citizens with democratic aspirations. Democracy cannot be reimagined by excluding those who have not had the opportunity to experience it. Moreover, democracy cannot exist in the imagination of the West only. Therefore, I interviewed citizens in China and Russia. I chose these countries because they are both major forces in global politics yet typically are excluded from discourses on democracy. Any country may undergo a level of authoritarianism in its form of governance. Democracies in the West have had their share of authoritative rulers, and several have emerged out of dictatorships to reclaim democracy. The citizens of authoritarian regimes have a democratic future, and they should have a say in it.

3. My final focus was attempted but failed democracies. In most of these cases, it was not easy for me to travel to these countries, and identifying or interviewing people from these countries presented a danger to them and me. For example, even if I were able to set up interviews in Syria or Afghanistan, the task of networking, obtaining translators, and conducting the interviews would be difficult, would draw too much attention, and would probably not yield meaningful responses from people who felt endangered. So I decided to work with refugees from those countries. I worked with local embassies and refugee centers in countries that maintain an entry port to the European Union,

where frequently refugees flee. I interviewed refugees from Afghanistan, Iran, Syria, Albania, Egypt, Ghana, and Pakistan and used translators provided by refugee centers and embassies to conduct the interviews in the refugees' native language when necessary.

This was a complex yet fascinating journey. The interviews frequently felt like democracy confessionals. People spoke plainly and earnestly about what troubled them. There were common threads, articulated in ways reflective of distinct cultural traditions of expression. I spoke with people whose politics are deeply conservative and others whose politics are fiercely progressive; young people who are enthusiastic and deeply cynical at the same time; older adults who are calm, disappointed, nostalgic, and hopeful. Many drew a distinction between democracy as an ideal and how it is practiced by governments. Capitalism and stakeholder interests frequently prevail. People often talked in the abstract, without referring to specific politicians. This is because they see the same problems continue despite transitions in governance and elected officials. It is clear that people have faith in democracy but little faith in elected officials, the media, or technology. What is particularly moving is how introspective informants get when asked about what might make democracy better. They point to local success stories of connection and expression and seem to be most energized by local governance. When drawing connections to elected officials and national or global forms of governance, informants often seem to indicate that to be sustained, democracy must also be restrained somehow. Corruption, capitalism, lack of immediate contact with politicians, and distaste for media coverage are all identified as things that get in the way of democracy working as it should. Citizens discuss local governance, the ability to do simple things well in everyday life, civic responsibility for fellow citizens, compassion, and empathy when considering good citizenship. Better access to information through media and technology, more immediate access to forms of governance, and equality in representation are recurring themes when they are asked about what might make democracy better. Responses surprised me with their mix of skepticism and hope.

In the interviews, people often gave textbook definitions of democracy, and when that happened I would ask again, hoping to get their own subjective read. When defining citizenship or democracy, participants often asked, "Did I get it right?" Often I would see blank stares from people who had hoped for democracy in their countries and were forced to abandon everything and leave in the midst of war. I am grateful that people allowed me to look into their eyes as they told me the poignant stories of fleeing one's own country so as to not be recruited by the Taliban. I chose to conduct interviews because I was interested in the aspirational. I wanted to have conversations with people who were willing to consider the question "What if?" with me. If things could be different, what might they look like? My purpose was to find what might improve and possibly follow democracy. The title of the book, *After Democracy*, invites readers to think about what might be. Interviews are often criticized as offering little beyond aspirational evidence. In this case, this was an asset. I used three broad questions as a way to start a conversation with participants and to get them to tell their own stories. Stories are personal. They look to the past and the future; they are nostalgic and aspirational. My companions in these conversations came from different cultures, and my task was to find out what unites them when they are asked to imagine a different democracy or what might follow democracy. But I was also curious about where they diverged in their opinions and why.

I was not the first in asking these questions. The sociologist Nina Eliasoph spent a few years studying how people talked or avoided talking about politics in small groups. People spoke "about politics backstage, in hushed tones," she remarked, as she began to trace a culture that prized interest politics and conversational politeness in ways that inadvertently reproduced apathy. In *Avoiding Politics: How Americans Produce Apathy in Everyday Life*, Eliasoph challenged the myth of apathy by looking for it where it was least likely to exist and thus provided a compelling explanation of how apathy is produced.[9] She employed a combination of conversational, interviewing, and observational techniques to conduct an ethnography of postsuburban civic groups. Her work is central to understanding how the structure of conversations and the failure to distinguish between civility and politeness in U.S. politics often prevent us from having poignant but important conversations.

I thought more about how to draw the political out of my conversational companions without provoking it. The political scientist Jane Mansbridge has already produced a groundbreaking, influential volume on what democracy might look like, were it imagined otherwise. She infiltrated and studied two micro-democracies, one functioning within the meetings of a small New England town and the second in an urban crisis center.[10] More recently, the legendary sociologist Arlie Hochschild set out to understand the roots of Tea Party conservative politics by immersing herself in that culture and, in so doing, unraveled the complex feelings of people who felt alienated in their own country. She described them as "strangers in their own land" and inadvertently untangled the political circumstances that led to Donald Trump becoming president in the United States.[11] The political scientist Kathy Cramer had deep conversations with Wisconsin voters in rural areas, to trace how economic insecurity ended up fostering a culture that both opposed and reelected big government.[12] Similarly, the sociologist Francesca Polletta, in *Freedom Is an Endless Meeting*, drew from interviews with activists in the United States to make concrete suggestions about how democratic cultures of participation could be reinvented.[13]

I studied these works to understand why and how they attained greater relevance. They gained meaning not only because they focused on a detailed study of a small community but also because their authors worked meticulously to connect these local trends to broader cultures of discontent. They did so through interpreting findings, using theory, and connecting their work to broader research. They were insightful; they were also driven by an emphasis on U.S.-based practices of democracy that my work seeks to move beyond. Yet we did not invent democracy in the United States, and we have not been practicing it for the longest. There are some problems in U.S.-based democracies that we encounter in other countries, and there are other problems that are entirely our own. Most recently, the Canadian politician and academic Michael Ignatief, utilizing his networks and access to a smaller subset of countries and cultures, produced his treatise on the ordinary virtues that define our times.[14] I would like to follow a similar approach of working within and beyond the West, to find out what unites us and separates us when we talk about democracy.

So I traced the conversational patterns that those who had traveled down these paths before had unraveled. I learned from the way they approached people, gained their trust, got them to open up and to engage in conversation that, I hoped, would be fulfilling for both of us. I used a combination of stratification and snowballing techniques to attain my group of democracy conversational companions. I organized my potential population into groups, divided by country. Within each country, I utilized my networks and asked them to introduce me to people who would not ordinarily cross my path of academics, teachers, students, or faculty. I further pursued the casual conversations that we start with strangers, while waiting at a busy café or as co-passengers on an airplane. I stopped and talked to the people we casually discount in our daily routines: security personnel, janitorial staff, civil service clerks, volunteers at civic organizations, and people working at the supermarket checkout register. Needless to say, I picked the timing and occasion for my conversation so as not to intrude on my participants' daily routines. I did not approach them and directly ask them what they think of democracy, although that would have made for an interesting experiment and possibly a different book. I began a casual conversation, and as rapport developed, my questions became more specific. This served two purposes. First, it created a comfortable zone for conversation and interaction. It permitted me to see whether these folks had an interest in chatting and whether there was room for me to request that I have a more focused conversation with them. Second, this practice permitted me to get a feel for my participants' politics, orientation, and general mind-set. I did not want to collect information about their political history or standard socio-demographic data. That is not what this study is about. This work is about conversation as a tool for learning about democracy. But I wanted to have some way of ascertaining that my snowballing strategy would generate a diverse sample. As I talked to people, asked to be introduced to their friends, and further expanded my conversational networks, I was thus able to ensure that I was generating a set of interviews with individuals from diverse backgrounds, occupations, and generations.

The Digital Question

The events of the past few decades underscore how central media are to democracy.[15] The work of social scientists has long tracked the relationship between technology, politics, and democracy over the past couple of decades. Recent waves of digitally aided unfinished revolutions, interrupted movements, and burgeoning populism have both excited us and disappointed us. They have filled us with hope about the digital pathways to democracy that technology avails; they have also made us aware of the vulnerability of these pathways.[16] They excited us with visions of democracy and also disappointed us when these visions were polluted with populism. We are accustomed to blaming technology for these problems. Elections are hacked into, populism is digitally propagated, hate speech prevails online, movements thrive online but rarely move offline, and the internet pulls us together but also further drives us apart.

There is truth to these claims. Still, what if we have been expecting something that digital technology is simply not able to provide? What if democracy is not the end goal but the path to something better, and what if technology can help us get closer to that?

This book is a response to the present condition. It emerges out of our long journey with democracy and our struggle with technology. These informal conversations with citizens from failed, aspiring, and flawed democracies are designed to give voice to people's stories about democracy. The political scientist Stephen Coleman has written extensively about our attempts to fix systemic problems of inequality with technology. In one of his most insightful books, titled *How Voters Feel*, he cleverly isolated the root of the problem: voters are being counted, but they are not feeling like their own votes count. The biggest problems that need fixing are not digital. Technology is not a Band-Aid. It is not a solution and frequently becomes a distraction from the deeper problems. This is why I chose not to ask my conversational companions about technology unless they chose to take the conversation there. I decided to let this book be about what people want democracy to look like. This is a book about what people would do if they could reimagine democracy.

Still, there is a place for technology in a contemporary and future democracy. There is room for technology in what might follow democracy. In fact, that is precisely what technology offers: room, space, meaning-making place. It creates infrastructure, it creates spaces, and it hosts conversations. Chat rooms and platforms like Twitter, Reddit, and Facebook present such spaces.

The technologies of our ancestors were parks, agoras, arenas, cafés, theaters, letters, newspapers, television sets, radios. Several of those technologically reified spaces continue to be meaningful for us. It is important to understand that architecture sets the tone, creates atmosphere, influences mood. Architecture also opens up possibilities for interaction and restricts others. Imagine conversations that take place in rooms with wide windows that let in natural light, with high ceilings that reflect the light and create a greater sense of space, and think about how this shifts your mood when participating in a conversation. By contrast, picture a dimly lit, smaller room, with no windows and low ceilings and with little personal space. Exciting conversations can take place in both spaces, but they take on different topics, texture, and tonality. Think about the design of a movie theater and how it demands our silence and attention once the movie begins. By contrast, bring to mind the small, loud, crowded corner dive bar you like to visit with friends, and think about how that space invites conversation of a different nature. That is how technology works. It sets the tone, and I am not at all sure that the internet, in its present form, is capable of setting the right tone for democracy.

As I explained earlier, technology is capable of doing many things, including making voices louder, but loud voices don't always lead to democracy. They often lead away from it. The sociologist Michael Schudson has famously argued that conversation, in fact, is not the soul of democracy.[17] Contrary to popular belief, there is no inherent democracy to the norms of conversation. By contrast, it is the institutions and norms of democracy that set the tone for a democratic conversation to happen, not the other way around. To paraphrase, yes, a conversation is not the soul of democracy, but perhaps it can be a way to find where that soul lies and reach it.

This book is about conversations. I already mentioned that technologies network us, but it's our stories that connect us, identify us, and, sometimes, divide us. So I would like to begin in reverse mode: figure out what these stories are, connect them, and in so doing also trace how technology can be designed to help us tell the stories that connect us, identify us, and do not divide us. Some things in life are fascinating because no matter where in the world you look for them, you know that they will be there and that they will the same, or similar: the sun, the moon, the sea. And there are things in life that are fascinating because they are different from every angle. Democracy is one of them.

TWO

Democracy on the Run

What is democracy? A deep silence trails this question when posed to people I converse with. More often than not, my informants pause for thought when asked to explain what, in their mind, is a democracy. Context does not seem to play a part here. People across all countries I visited tend to pause, think, and frequently revert to textbook definitions of democracy. Perhaps this is because we are accustomed to identifying what is not democratic in our search for pure democracy. We recognize democracy by reminding ourselves of what it is not. The conditions, the examples, and the very vocabulary for describing what is *not* democratic come to us more easily. When asked what something is, we fall into the habit of defining it by what it is not. Voice and equality are prominent themes that emerge as my conversational companions and I delve into this question together.

One would think that a concept that has lived with us for thousands of years would be easy to define. On the other hand, it is not uncommon for people to want for words that describe the familiar. Ask yourself what friendship, family, love, work, death, or life mean to you, and you might be met with the same initial inner silence. Pause for thought does not imply that we don't know what these things mean. Yet these are big questions about everyday things that often blend ordinary routines with extraordinary expectations. How do we find the words to describe things that we recognize by feeling?

And so democracy is one of those things that feels right when it manages to reconcile ordinary routines with extraordinary expectations. Pause for thought is common when the question is posed. This is not a new feeling. It is not specific to this generation. It is not unique to our era, and it does not characterize a particular region of the world. The question has puzzled scientists, philosophers, and citizens for ages. Thomas More wrote *Utopia* out of a longing for this perfect state of being, driven by a democratically imagined world.[1] He wrote two books in Latin, the first one focused around questions of time. The second, carrying the title *Utopia*, was written from the perspective of a traveler who returned to England to report on life in this exotically thought-up society. When I first imagined this book, I wanted to write a contemporary version of *Utopia*. The root of the word is Greek, yet we use it quite differently than Greeks did, in contemporary and ancient times. In Greece, ουτοπία is a term used to describe an ideal state of being, desired yet forever out of reach. We use the term often to label concepts that are dreamy but deeply unrealistic, and we tend to use it dismissively. The term communicates a slightly more optimistic outlook when employed colloquially in the English-speaking world. It is telling, therefore, that More wrote a text about democracy and titled it *Utopia*. He wrote about the promise and peril of democracy, aware that the condition he was describing might be forever unattainable. More lived under a monarchy, and his book was published in 1516. He was ambivalent about the possibility of finding utopia within a democratic state of governance. His prominent role in the monarchy, together with his life, ended when he was convicted of treason and beheaded for refusing to accept King Henry VIII as the head of the Church of England, in 1535.

In *Utopia*, there are many terms, including the name of the book's protagonist, that hint at the impossibility of the task More took on. More, speaking through his protagonist, Rafael Hythloday, a philosopher whose last name derives from Greek and roughly translates as a "peddler of nonsense," refers to Plato in explaining that "as long as everyone has his own property, there is no hope of curing them and putting society back into good condition."[2] More was uncertain as to whether property ownership was compatible with democracy, yet worried that the lack of property ownership stripped all motives for profit and general well-being. On the same page, More, a fictional character who happens to share the same name as the *Utopia* author, adds that "no one can live comfortably where everything is held in common. For how can there be an abundance of goods when everyone stops working because he is no longer motivated by making a profit, and grow lazy because he relies on the labors of others."[3] The clever character play associated the different opinions to separate characters, but it is clear that they reflect the ambivalence that drives More's own thinking. Not only do these thoughts sound familiar, but also they presciently anticipate the ideological struggle between capitalism and communism—similar to Plato and Aristotle, centuries ago.

Plato, in the *Republic*, considered property ownership less than ideal to the condition of the republic. Unlike Plato, Aristotle offered an argument in support of private ownership and the path to liberty in *Politics*. These points are often extracted from context and presented as the opposite. The relation of property ownership to equality resurfaces in all the sciences, in all religions despite their origin, and in most everyday conversations about all things, political or not. What is mine versus what is yours, to put it plainly, is the primal barrier that preempts any conversation about the public good. We have been having the same conversations for centuries, using different languages, terms, and perspectives. I have always interpreted these two arguments as reflective of the ambivalence the condition of democracy invites and not as two opposing opinions. They are part of a longer conversation, and for me, they are reflective of many paths to democracy.

More had many other opinions that he illustrated within a fantastical context. This book is not fantasy, but I hope it resonates with the conversational tone in *Utopia*, because conversation leads to specific examples in the context of reality. Abstract definitions frequently fail when put to this test. I am not alone in making this point. Alexis de Tocqueville marveled at the triumphs but also anticipated many of the failures of democracy.[4] He was vexed about the tyranny and the triumph of the majority, a concern that surfaced in my conversations with people across continents. Jean-Jacques Rousseau notoriously complained about disinterested citizens who threatened the potency of democracy.[5] Declining levels of participation from voters are a feature of current elections around the world. John Dewey and Walter Lippmann had their own debate about whether citizens can individually manage democracy or whether they are forever doomed to be manipulated by elites. Lippmann was an award-winning writer, journalist, public intellectual, and famous extrovert. In *Public Opinion*, published in the 1920s, he eloquently argued that democracy does not scale up. The founding fathers of the United States crafted a democracy formed around smaller communities of people, where it was possible to attain expert knowledge on public affairs and communicate directly with designated officials. Modern societies have scaled up to representative democracies, where it is difficult for citizens to stay informed and make knowledgeable decisions. So citizens must rely on knowledge elites to guide them, yet at the same time, they are susceptible to the manipulation of these elites.

Lippmann was a flamboyant, social, and quick-witted character who spent most of his time in Manhattan, a sharp contrast to the more introverted John Dewey, who was a psychologist, philosopher, education reformer, and introspective public intellectual. Dewey was among the first to applaud Lippmann's lucid critique of democracy. Still, he had his own take on the matter and found that with the right form of educational, social, and civic preparations, publics could resist manipulation from the elites. Both were idealists who deeply believed in the democratic condition. They saw the democratic condition as central to the human condition. Dewey famously said, "Democracy and the one, ultimate, ethical ideal of humanity are to my mind synonymous."[6] Lippmann did not disagree but was deeply concerned about the increasing role media played in helping people learn about events that they could not directly experience. He famously drew a distinction between the world outside and the pictures in our heads, to explain the difference between what actually happens and what we find out happened through the media we rely on.

It is true that contemporary media further complicate these questions. They seem to widen the distance between public and private, citizens and politicians. Elected officials perform highly rehearsed public personas online, on TV, and in the general press that only leave citizens more skeptical, cynical, and detached from the business of politics.[7] Polling mechanisms, including big-data quantifications, turn nuanced civic opinions into *numbered voices*, quantified opinions or visualizations meant to generate support for one policy proposal or the other.[8] Newer media open up new opportunities for engaging citizens and listening to them.[9] They are rarely used to these ends, however, by politicians and citizens who misunderstand or exploit the internet.[10] The internet will not democratize, equalize, or create a robust public sphere. The Gutenberg press, letter writing (a popular form of conveying the news prior to newspapers), newspapers, radio, TV, and photojournalism, to name a few, did not manage to do so before. These media pluralize voices, make democracy more porous, and open up public spaces for conversation, each in their own way. The internet, in particular, hints at new models of governance that we might begin to explore, if only we give up on retrofitting it to support systems it was not meant to correct.

Humanity has never experienced what we may understand as a perfect democratic condition. Smaller, direct democracies had their problems, which lingered and evolved into more complex problems as democracy scaled up and evolved into a variety of forms, direct and representative, including parliamentary, consensus, liberal, social, deliberative, presidential, and more authoritarian modalities of democracy that include voting but restrict choice. This is a normal situation; it has never been possible to define democracy, and it has always been difficult to put it to work. Yet we have always been quick to assume that somewhere, somehow, in an elusive collective past, someone got this right, and we are the doomed ones now, left to live with the remnants of what once may have been a glorious democracy.

I begin from this theoretical promise to unlock a subjunctive modality of politics, a potential phantasmagoria of democracy—to trace ghosts of democracy's past; to track dreams of democracy's future; to record fears, hopes, and missed opportunities; to travel along with others down paths of regret and nostalgia and turn them into creative emotion that can navigate us into something different. "Survivors of the twentieth century," the scholar and playwright Svetlana Boym proclaims in contemplating the future of nostalgia, "we are all nostalgic for a time when we were not nostalgic."[11] I am not interested in finding a way back to that time. So I begin by inviting people to go back to the original question: *What is democracy?* In posing this question, I am aware that we cannot escape our nostalgia. I hope that I can tap into the connective consciousness of nostalgia and invite people to have a conversation with me about defining democracy that is inclusive of what it is, what it has been, and what it might be.

How do crowds turn into masses, and, to paraphrase Hannah Arendt, how do masses turn into democracies?[12] What are democracies, is it possible to measure them, and is democracy indeed possible around the world? Conversations in this book attempt to discuss democracy as an idea and an ideal. Crucial to the problem of democracy are the concepts of equality and freedom—that is, autonomy: the kind of freedom that does not disrespect the rights of others or constrain our own.[13] That is the promise of democracy. But is it a feasible promise? Is it democracy that must change, or is it us? Preliminary findings suggest that most respondents have faith in the condition of democracy. It is the ability of their governments to put it to work that they gravely doubt. It is this growing skepticism around the art of government that makes them feel that, even when cast, their vote rarely matters.

Much of the history of democracy has been focused around the right to vote. But once the right to vote is obtained and equally accessed, citizens find that it is not enough. Citizens require equal access to information and to the tools with which to interpret information to make choices that represent them in the long term. The right to vote is a necessary yet not sufficient condition. The right to an informed vote emerges as a condition that all contemporary democracies must guarantee. My conversational companions frequently make distinctions between misinformation, or inaccurate information, and disinformation, or information aimed at manipulating beliefs. They seem disappointed that the civic environment, in which they come into being as citizens, is plagued by both. Equality, voice, access, a vote—these are all constant refrains as these conversations dissolve into themes.

Inspired by theory and everyday conversation, I synthesize these responses to the question of democracy. They cover multiple terrains, to examine the architecture of freedom, what it means to have equal access to opportunity, freedom as an adventure, shared fantasies, fictions of play, populist forays into the democratic, and the scenography of democratically informed technology.[14] So here are themes that emerge in conversation on what democracy has, should have, and might have been, in these polyphonic, multicultural, and geographically dispersed yet interconnected exchanges about the many what-ifs of democracy.

Silence and Noise

Following warm-up banter with my conversational companions, I ask, "What is democracy?" Most often, I am met with a pause. Eyes shift away from what was previously direct contact. Some smile nostalgically. Others nod and ponder in silence for a minute. Some make a sarcastic gesture, affectively nodding at the impossibility of the question. I want to interpret this silence as an initial response, as it is significant. As scientists, we often record what we are told, and we are curious about what is left unsaid. This silence is a sign to be interpreted. It is indicative of a variety of different moods, dispositions, or affects to the question. Louis, my first interview, a cab driver in Mexico City, pauses and shoots me a sly eye roll through the rearview mirror before he takes a minute to respond.

Mujahid, a young man in his mid-twenties from Afghanistan, lives in refugee lodgings set up in Greece. He meets me in the classroom at a school he is attending to improve his foreign-language skills. The program is funded by European Union refugee-allotted funds. I ask him what democracy is; I also feel foolish at the same time for asking because he has just explained that his family is still in Afghanistan. He left because staying meant joining the Taliban. Not joining meant being killed and putting his family in danger from the Taliban. Yet he has volunteered to talk with me about democracy. His glance is both poignant and optimistic, as my question to him is also met with this initial silence.

I meet Valeria, a Belarussian and Russian photojournalist in St. Petersburg. She is also an artist, delving into photography mostly and with an eye toward a possible exhibition soon. Valeria is gleefully describing how she spent some time drifting about and taking photos at Nevsky Prospect, the busy and renowned boulevard of a city that is destroyed and rebuilt as part of its core identity. She tells me this story of how she came across an acoustic guitar, seemingly abandoned on the pavement, resting against a streetlamp. Nikolai Gogol had famously written of the Nevsky, "It deceives at all hours, the Nevsky Prospect does, but most of all when night falls . . . when the devil himself lights the streetlamps to show everything in false colors."[15] As I mentioned earlier, the guitar appears stranded but attracts interest from passersby as Valeria photographs it. People approach it, examine it, as she photographs it further, but no one appears to be its rightful owner. As she leaves, out of the corner of her eye, she notices someone run up and grab it. It is unclear whether he was the owner either, but it is clear that the value of the guitar has appreciated by virtue of being photographed. With this story as a backdrop, I ask, "So what is democracy?" Laughter ensues, musing, silence.

This silence follows me as I continue to travel and strike up conversations. I am met with silence from Matthias, an unemployed gamer I interview in Germany; Aras, a Turkish immigrant driver I interview in Berlin; and Barbara, a service-industry worker I interview in Dresden. Berlin and Dresden are cities with their own bittersweet histories of things lost, gained, and rebuilt. It becomes obvious that the silence that trails this first question is not specific to one region either. It emerges as an initial response across all regions covered. In the United States, people pause, ponder, then throw the question back at me with a "Hmmmm . . . what *is* democracy?" In Russia, I sometimes get nervous laughter, sometimes a serious stare. In Greece, I sense an obligation to define democracy; Greeks often feel the weight of history on their contemporary shoulders, and this defines how they respond to many questions of everyday life. In China, I sense an earnestness and a hesitation to respond to the question, and sometimes I also receive a bitterness with some sarcasm thrown in. At the refugee centers, I am greeted with a different kind of silence when I ask this question. It is the silence you get from people who have seen a lot and are in no mood to play know-it-alls.

There are different kinds of silence. Silence certainly doesn't indicate the lack of a ready response or disinterest. Silence is not the absence of an opinion. It can mean many things. In this case, silence is first embedded within the difficulty we have had, throughout the long history of humanity, of defining and applying democracy. Further, it reflects the need to think beyond the stereotypical response and give me answers that really mean something. I appreciate that about my respondents. Additionally, silence conveys cultural differences in processes of thinking through big questions, like the one I am asking. I confess that I find this silence beguiling. The absence of an immediate response gives me time to spy on my respondents' reactions: to observe, record, and interpret what lies beneath the silence. As I wait, I watch for affective expressions: gestures, eye movement, tiny facial contortions, changes in body posture. It is a privilege to be able to observe and interpret silence.

All too often, we hurry to characterize silence as reluctance or absence of a particular position on an issue. We also assume that prolonged silence might communicate apathy. As social scientists, we know that silence also conveys oppression. But the easy assumption, in matters of politics, is to interpret silence as abstention, absence, apathy. Not voting, for instance, is an example of silence. "I vote so that I can have the right to an opinion, the right to complain," exclaims Jessica. We observe declining numbers of participation in elections globally, and we distinguish between a vocal public, those who voted, and an apathetic, disinterested, and thus silent public, those who did not vote. Yet silence is an opinion. It is the expression of many possible opinions, in fact. It is an expression of opinions that possibly do not fit into the prescribed and limited options that referenda and elections present for us. It is a political stance. The absence of opinion is, in fact, an expression of a political position. It communicates refusal, discontent, indignation, and indecision. All of these are valid political positions that send a message, one that the conventional processes of democracy and politicking ignore, for they are trained to turn their attention to the voices who did not employ silence and voted. Silence is as important as voice, however. We habitually listen to voice, but we must train the ear to listen to silence, to observe it, to interpret what lies behind it, and above all, to register it as political.

In the sciences, we have many theories as to what invites this silence. The condition of contemporary democracy is a popular trope of discussion for politicians, media analysts, and the public. In synthesizing scientific and popular perspectives, in previous work and prior to conducting these interviews, I have identified five conditions that characterize most democracies. I see nostalgia for the past forms of political engagement, frequently wrapped in rhetoric that idealizes past iterations of a public sphere.[16] I see limitations to civic involvement imposed by the representative democracy model, as it functions in a mass society resting on a capitalist economy.[17] I see the aggregation of public opinion within representative democracy models through polling.[18] I see declining civic participation through formal channels of political involvement.[19] And I see the growth of public cynicism and disillusionment toward politics and the mass media.[20] These five tendencies characterize contemporary democracies, describe civic engagement in mass societies, and situate the media in the overall equation. I first wrote about these tendencies over twenty years ago.[21] I do not find that any of these conditions have changed, and I think it important that they premise any conversation I have about what democracy means today.

I argue that many of us often tend to interpret silence as political apathy because, in our collective imaginations of the past, we have rendered the progression through eras populated by citizens much more active than we are. And yet a careful historical examination reveals that citizens of the past not only were as likely to be inactive but were as likely to be baffled by the condition of democracy as we are. They were willing to accept it as an abstraction, flexibly negotiated across societies. We are quick to interpret the (silent) modern citizens as passive, cynical, and disconnected. They very well may be, but these trends are not specific to our era.[22] Our nostalgia for past civic eras that never existed creates a feedback loop that can only lead to further disillusionment.

What is amplified in our era, however, is what many observers identify as the democratic paradox. Many people want the immediacy that direct democracy provides. Yet this immediacy is not only absent but also impossible within the mass scale of representative democracies. Democracy promises pluralism, but it cannot deliver it on a mass scale.[23] Representative democracy reinforces homogeneity of opinion through majority rule, and this, by definition, precludes any possibility of a true and pure plurality of voice. Civic engagement is possible, but most democracies are not pure democracies— they are instead a compromise. In Germany, I spent time interviewing and wandering about with people in Dresden and Berlin, both cities trapped, liberated, and redefined through historical circumstance.

In Dresden, folks speak with me about the total destruction of the city during World War II and the processes through which cultural identity was preserved as the restructuring occurred. Some of the conversations echo my experience in St. Petersburg, a city that experienced a similar level of destruction and reconstruction during the same era. My conversational companions joke with me that they are too far out east for their TVs to capture broadcast signals of Western programs that the more proximate Berliners enjoy. As we warm up to conversation, their comments oscillate between a dislike for and yet a need for compromise. Their sense of being embeds an understanding that compromise is both a curse and a condition for democracy. In commenting about everyday politics, it is clear that they are displeased with how compromise necessitates an inclusion of extremist points of view into governance, points of view that are often not compatible with democratic principles. Compromises are important in democracies, concludes Lenora, an administrative assistant from Germany.

The process of compromise that drives representative democracies is augmented by the culture of polling. The tendency to aggregate public opinion as a way to easily estimate what citizens think inflates certain points of view, disadvantages others, and leads us down irreversible paths to misinformation and disinformation, as we witnessed in recent elections and referenda.[24] The political scientist Susan Herbst long ago described this trend as a process that produces "numbered voices."[25] She explained that polling exchanges the individuality, detail, and authenticity of personal opinion on public affairs for a concentration of opinions that fit into predetermined question-and-answer sets reported in aggregation. The tendency to limit the kinds of questions citizens are asked and the range of responses that they are given limit citizen engagement. People are not invited to deliberate but merely asked to report agreement or disagreement with questions, in ways that render them indistinguishable from bots. Polling failed in predicting the outcome of the U.S. presidential election in 2016 and further misinformed projections on the Brexit referendum, as well as the Grexit referendum before it. Not even the most sophisticated, micro-targeted statistical models were able to offer accurate predictions when the data analyzed were based on such simplistic ways of inquiring what was on the public's mind.[26]

Yet media and politicians continue to rely on polling to justify political decisions. This insistence only serves to widen the distance between media, politicians, and publics. Why participate in polling processes that will only be later manipulated to justify a political agenda? Cynicism toward media and politicians is reinforced and reproduced through the exploitation of public opinion. Research on cynicism has long revealed that the language employed by politicians and the media, the tendency to focus on insider goings-on instead of straightforward reporting, leads to irreversible skepticism.[27] Cynicism is often presented as a performative stance, a mask used to conceal powerless and limited opportunities for engagement.[28]

So the silence that greets my big first question—"What is democracy?"—is the result of a long process of nostalgia, disillusionment, and cynicism that shrouds any question about democracy. It is a silence that has been ignored for some time and a silence few people have the interest or the ability to listen to. And finally, it is a silence that gains gravitas as it is pitted against the noise that surrounds the conversations I have.

What is the noise of the present moment that renders this silence even more powerful as a symbolic statement? It is the culmination of factors that led me to write this book and to select the countries I visited. For Greece, the noise that surrounds this silence is the long history of a country that invented democracy but has one of the shortest track records practicing it. It is the noise of a country that transitioned through six prime ministers in the past ten years, each anointed by European Union officials and begrudgingly voted into office by the public. In the United Kingdom, it is the noise of ambitious politicians who posed a complex question about leaving the European Union mostly as a way to distract people from other, deeper social problems. They then asked for a yes-or-no response, received a result they did not expect, and then abandoned the ship as new captains boarded to head down an impossible path of negotiation.

In Germany, this silence is the noise of a country that is seemingly prosperous and has imposed its financial ethos on the European Union, through several financial bailout packages negotiated for bankrupt E.U. partner countries. Behind the prosperity lie smaller salaries and reduced benefits, divides between Eastern and Western cultures that persist, xenophobia, the ghost of neofascism, and prime ministers who strike costly compromises between the extreme left and extreme right to maintain a politics of the center. The United States finds itself more networked than ever, yet disconnected by the stories people share via these networks. Unsure of its identity and uncertain of its future, the United States finds itself in a condition that it had only observed other nations go through in the past but never expected to endure. Brazil has also suffered through a sequence of prime ministers indicted for fraud, to the point where both accusers and accused have now committed fraud at some point in their political careers.

Mexico, during the time I was conducting interviews, was anticipating elections, to vote out a leader who swayed publics with populist rhetoric only to disappoint while in office. Russia is the land of Vladimir Putin, a leader the rest of the world demonizes without recalling the context under which he rose to power. Mikhail Gorbachev is given credit for ushering in perestroika, but he left or was driven out of office quickly, to be succeeded by Boris Yeltsin, a leader whose tenure left a massive country to be run by the mafia and with increasing crime rates. While none of my respondents were blind to the manner with which Putin has held on to power, they remembered what Russia looked like before he ascended to power. China is another country that Western democracies tend to dismiss as authoritarian. Respondents were deeply aware of the limited choices they were given within the context of a so-called democracy. One has to ask: Are the choices we are given in Western democracies that much more diverse? And finally, there are the many abandoned homes of the refugees. All are places where Western democracies, in the name of liberty and profit, interfered, made a mess, ruined people's lives, packed up and left when resources ran low, left conditions unbearable for those left behind, and then imposed limits on where and how in the world they might seek refuge.

That is the noise. Wouldn't you want a moment of silence, in the midst of all that?

Familiarity and Ambivalence

Once we move past the pensive silence, respondents begin to freestyle and riff on familiar tropes on what democracy means. I frequently receive answers that echo textbook definitions from high school and college, reproduce popular slogans, and employ a common vernacular. Khrilid, a refugee from Morocco, tells me that democracy is about the law of the people, voting, having people choose. Nikos, from Greece, tells me that it is about the fundamental human right to speak and be heard among equals. Xheni, a refugee from Albania, drops "freedom" and "transparency" as the first words that come to mind. Drew, from New York, explains that it is about inclusion, respect, and a shared set of values. Mujahid, a refugee from Afghanistan, talks about majority rule and justice. Victor, from Russia, adds that democracy is about freedom of thought and freedom of speech. Concerned that he is providing textbook definitions in response to this question, Nathan from Canada finally concludes, "[Democracy] is like the air I breathe."

The civic vocabulary of democracy is founded on the constructs of freedom, equality, and fraternity. Applied to everyday life, these further evoke the protection of fundamental human and civil rights; equal access to opportunity and voice; and decision-making processes that are just, transparent, representative of a majority, and directed toward protecting the common good. The concept is simple enough when we think about interaction in small groups. Within smaller groups, such issues emerge but are often resolved through quick conversation. Deliberation, frequently employed as a path for resolving disagreements within representative democracies, might even be considered an overproduction in such cases. As democracies scale up in size, context, and complexity, freedom, equality, and fraternity become inaccessible to some people. Protection of fundamental rights, equal access, and transparent and just representation involve overlapping yet distinct constituencies with differences that are frequently insurmountable. Democracy is a way to reconcile differences while ensuring that the greater good will be preserved. Yet the smaller republics of the Greco-Roman period were not simple enough to escape these conflicts, and the larger republics of the contemporary era still struggle with the modern reincarnation of difference. The political theorist Sheldon Wolin once wrote, "Democracy is too simple for complex societies and too complex for simple ones."[29] My participants resort to familiar language that reflects the aspirational thinking that we all share when we dream about democracy. Still, ambivalence lies beneath the familiar.

On a walk along the promenade, Cristina from Ecuador, presently living in Greece, says that democracy does not really exist, because it is constantly confined by context. She compares her experience of growing up in Ecuador to living in the United States and then moving to Greece. The similarity is striking. Democracy appears to be both present and absent across all contexts. "It is whatever you want it to be," she says. It is how we put it to work that restricts or empowers us. As we walk by skateboarders doing ollies by a statue of Alexander the Great, prominently displayed on the promenade of Thessaloniki, Greece, I am reminded of my first interview on the other side of the world, in the crowded streets of Mexico City in midday rush hour. Louis, a cab driver in his early fifties, never actually told me what democracy is. "What *is* democracy?" he exclaimed, as he went on to discuss what it's not. It is not about the privileged few having access to power, it is not about having too few parties, and it is not about "power being distributed in only a few hands." He talked about people coming and going through offices of government without effecting any real change or restructuring habits that are both old and old-fashioned; then he came to this conclusion: "On cover, it's democracy, but it does not feel like it."

Ambivalence prevails as my conversational companions move beyond the core concepts of democracy. "It's called democracy, but it's really not," are the final words I get from Khrilid. "It all depends on what the government does with it," says Lucian from Syria. The multilingual and polyphonic testimonies coalesce around this theme, as Nikos adds, "On paper, we have democracy, . . . but it is difficult to have democracy in our era." Everyone seems to understand what democracy is, but nobody appears to think that it exists.

After a certain point, I begin to wonder whether I will ever have a conversation with someone who tells me that democracy is alive and well, and can be located at coordinate x. "Democracy should be ideal, but it is not," says Xheni, a refugee from Albania, and Dimitris from Greece explains to me that democracy is a beautiful idea, not to be found in reality. Either we all define democracy in a way that renders it unattainable, or we appear to live in a world where democracy is on the run—perhaps a little bit of both, I jot down.

A few days later, I speak with Uzma, a refugee from Pakistan, who possesses a very sharp understanding of what democracy should be. He speaks with me about the value of being able to provide one's consent on a policy that affects one, on choosing freely, and on being able not just to place someone in office but also to remove those who do not serve the public good. But he is concerned that this understanding of what exactly constitutes the "public good" is increasingly muddied by populist promises. "People go for fame," he tells me in English, "and the majority follows." Umair, another refugee from Pakistan, is sitting by him. He further talks about how populists prevail and voters are easily swayed as leaders make empty promises to bring jobs and prosperity to be elected into office. "People should think of the progress of the state, not just their own when voting," he tells me in the end. Populism becomes a persistent refrain during all my conversations around the world. I wonder whether it is truly possible for anyone to abandon any form of subjective volition and endorse the common good.

As I read over my notes and look for themes in how participants responded to my questions, a phrase by Sheldon Wolin becomes a synaptic refrain for me: "fugitive democracy." Wolin understood the *political* to be about the belief that a free society made out of difference could still strive for the common good through deliberation aimed at protecting the well-being of the collective. *Politics*, on the other hand, is about contestation, by the publics with unequal access to power, over access to resources. "Politics is continuous, ceaseless, and endless," he argues, whereas "the political is episodic, rare."[30] It would seem that the majority of people I converse with are trapped in politics but rarely experience the political.

Democracy, Wolin adds, is one out of many iterations of the political, and it happens to be the one idea that resonates the most among people. Wolin refuses to define it as a form of governance, preferring to describe it instead as "a project concerned with the political potentialities of ordinary citizens, that is, with their possibilities for becoming political beings through the self-discovery of common concerns and of modes of action for realizing them."[31] It would seem, then, that the responses to the question about democracy are about the collective imaginaries made out of all of these individually articulated what-ifs. It is problematic to make democracy work when we understand it as a form of governance. It is a way of being political, and it is a way of being human. Naturally, it is both, present and absent, abstract and unrealizable, evoked in conversations across geolocal boundaries yet difficult to locate, for "[democracy] is not about where the political is located but how it is experienced."[32] Wolin arrives at this conclusion following a thorough, precise, and succinct overview of both theories and past states of democracy. This is not a statement that he makes lightly. He does not provide an explicit definition for the wonderful phrase "fugitive democracy," to my chagrin, letting us all think for ourselves about whether democracy can ever eventually help us think and act beyond boundaries. But he does introduce the phrase alongside a quote from Adam Ferguson's *An Essay on the History of Civil Society*: "Democracy seems to revive in a scene of wild disorder and tumult."[33] "Democracy is fractured," blurts out Daphne, a young freelance journalist from the United Kingdom, during one of my interviews, further validating this train of thought.

We have always assumed that democracy is a condition that thrives in and brings about peace. In our civic upbringing, democracy is collectively associated with a state of, at the very least, equilibrium. But in my conversations, that is rarely the case. It is constantly about disorder and tumult and does not necessarily provide a way out of these conditions. It is about silence, noise, and constant ambivalence. Perhaps democracy does have a fugitive soul, and perhaps, as I had originally set out to discover, it is not best understood as a form of governance but, rather, as a way of being.

Equality

Equal access to the right to vote, to opportunity, to the expression of opinions, to education, to choice, and to freedom routinely come up as respondents ponder the meaning of democracy. Once people get beyond the initial silence, and as they begin to toy with the ambivalence of a democracy that has always been fugitive, the first construct they identify is equality. It is fitting that as democracy is on the run, citizens seek stability around an idea they place at the core of democracy: equality. The long pauses in response to the question of democracy reflect uncertainty, thoughtfulness, and disenchantment. The tendency to latch onto formulaic definitions yet move beyond them at the same time reflects the difficulty of defining an ideal that will possibly remain fugitive. The logical process that follows in conversation is that equality can safeguard the fragility of democracy. And thus, equality emerges as the primary condition that can permit us to attain, at the very least, a cognitive hold on democracy.

In explaining what is meant by "equality," my conversational companions draw on a variety of big and loaded concepts. "Freedom of expression" is often brought up as a condition synonymous with "equality." It is as if equality cannot be imagined without freedom. Yet, in describing how equality and freedom coexist within a democracy, all folks draw from the idea of consensus or majority rule. Viktor, from Russia, tells me that democracy means to think freely and to speak freely. Fiona, from Albania, explains that democracy is about freedom, yes, but to justifiable ends. I ask what this means; she talks about being present, being alert, voicing concern about the important things, and making choices about what is important carefully. Drew, from the United States, immediately connects the idea of equality with that of respect for a set of commonly defined values. Simela, from Russia, tells me that freedom of expression is important because she grew up in a cultural context where this was not always possible. She adds, "Being able to express yourself freely is important, but it is not enough."

These responses dance around the familiar refrains of equality and freedom of speech that are commonly encountered in democracies. As democratic citizens, we are defined by our duty to speak freely and, in so doing, not to restrict the right of others to speak freely too. Thus, we must all have equal access to freedom of speech, even if this means that we often think twice about what we say to ensure that it does not encroach on the rights of others. Still, when the conversation stumbles on defining boundaries that guarantee equal access to freedom for all, the conversation gets complex, as one's aspirations of freedom may naturally clash with others' expectations of respect. We often bring up equality and freedom in tandem but in conversation realize that the two concepts restrict each other more often than not. We assume that equality is a necessary condition for freedom, and vice versa, only to realize later that they are necessary yet not sufficient. If we act freely as citizens, we will inadvertently produce inequalities through our actions. Likewise, by treating everyone equally, we may privilege points of view that threaten the freedom of others. We may also confuse equality with fairness, equivalence, egalitarianism, and several other synonymous ideas. What is equal is not always fair, and what is fair is often contextual. Equality does not guarantee difference, and neither does freedom. Further, great freedom often leads to greater pluralization but not necessarily better democracy.[34]

For political scientists and philosophers, the incompatibility between the concepts of freedom and equality is not a new question.

In fact, traditional, and potentially more conservative, philosophers and political scientists have considered freedom and equality as opposites. It is intriguing that we evoke them as companion concepts in our everyday lives. The philosopher Isaiah Berlin referred to the moral conflict between equality and freedom as "an intrinsic, irremovable element in human life."[35] It is part of our inescapable struggle with being human.

This book is not about how philosophers have explicated the moral conflicts presented by the way our societies define and practice freedom, equality, and democracy. It is about how people talk about these concepts in their everyday lives. It is important to acknowledge, however, that as societies, we have developed responses to some of these questions, solutions to some of these problems, and pathways out of conflicts that are recurring throughout the progression of humanity. In fact, the volume of work our scholarly endeavors have produced is awe-inspiring. There are few moral conflicts presented by our politicians, for instance, that have not been debated and, in most cases, resolved by scholars. Our societies have produced knowledge that is capable of addressing the moral conflicts of democracy; for a variety of reasons, discussed as conversations with my informants continue, this knowledge has not transformed into practice.

The question of equality is not new, yet it resurfaces across the ages in new contexts and is always defined by the sociocultural, geopolitical, and economic conditions that assign each era its own meaning. While the conceptual meaning of equality has remained the same, the idea has lent itself to different practices in ancient times, during the Middle Ages, and during the transition from an agricultural to an industrial society, to name a few eras. Although we have never gotten equality right, to put it plainly, our efforts have always been guided by the problems of the time.

The philosopher Elizabeth Anderson's work on equality considers our complicated struggles with equality and freedom and provides a response that is both compelling and relevant to the contemporary way of living.[36] Anderson has been working with and against conventional understandings of equality for the majority of her career. Her approach is relevant to our era, and to this book in particular, because it tackles the question of equality from the vantage point of value, instead of access. Anderson explains that while it is easy to agree on inequality, it is difficult to come to terms with what type of equality we want. My informants associate equality as the starting point of democracy, driven by the assumption that in pure democracy, we all begin from a common point of equal access. Yet, as Anderson clarifies, this is more limiting than empowering, as it restricts our ability to come up with corrective mechanisms when inequalities arise.[37] Further, equal access might guarantee a spot on the start line, but it does not necessarily lead to an equal path down to the finish line. The world is made up of people who are both unequal and different in countless ways; setting common standards does not ensure equality, nor is democracy about making sure all citizens fit into a prescribed equality mold. Further, in contemporary societies, people can exercise freedoms that permit them to claim different identities across domains of activity that overlap or are distinct, including work, home, the social sphere, interest groups, and several other public, private, or hybrid spheres of activity. Any relevant premise of equality must be inclusive of the contemporary character of identity. In a *New Yorker* article, Anderson presents her perspective on freedom and equality like this: "At church, I'm one thing. At work, I'm something else. I'm something else at home, or with my friends. The ability to not have an identity that one carries from sphere to sphere, but, rather, to be able to slip in and adopt whatever values and norms are appropriate while retaining one's identities in other domains? . . . That is what it is to be free. How do you build a society that allows for such variety without turning difference into a constraint?"[38]

The foundational assumption that we make about equality is one that drives us down the wrong path. We associate equality with democracy. That is not an incorrect assumption. We further presume that democracy leads to equality. This *is* an incorrect assumption. Equality derives from a distribution of value that is equitable. And therein lies the problem, because value has always been subjectively defined. While we do arrive at common understandings of what is valuable, these definitions are always contextually sensitive to the norms of a particular era. And they always will be. Value, equality, and democracy are all flexible concepts, even though we often pretend they are not. They are everlasting because they are ever changing. If they were rigid, they would not be able to evolve. Several of my informants acknowledge this. Nick from the United States, for instance, with a background in finance, pauses before he delivers a definition of democracy that deliberately avoids any mention of the political. He describes democracy as a form of social organization that aims to represent people better. Olga, a pharmacist from Greece, tells me that democracy is about arriving at a commonly shared set of values, and she describes this process as one that is a constant struggle toward understanding, redefining, and getting closer to that which is better.

What is understood as good, or better, is not fixed. It is specific to eras, contexts, and people. Anderson argues that we are running our societies, our democracies, and our general systems of governance on understandings of value that are no longer relevant. The first problematic assumption is that democracies can create equality. They cannot, because they are not value-trading entities. Market societies are and are thus able to define, allocate, assign, and distribute value in ways that can map the path to equality and strengthen democracy.

I simplify a nuanced argument that Anderson first made in her early work, on value in ethics and economics.[39] She explicated the difficulty of reconciling pluralism with value, by illustrating the distance between markets that operate on fairly fixed understandings of worth yet are driven by the behaviors of people who often judge value in subjective ways. My informants are acutely aware of how difficult it is to reconcile freedom and equality in a democracy. But several refer to equality in the abstract as if it were something that manifests itself or is somehow called into being in democratic societies. They do not bring up market societies until later on when I speak with them about how democracy might get better. Even then, they bring up corruption before they talk about capitalism.

Anderson finds that we need not give up on a market society or democracy, as long as we recognize the limitations of both and come up with corrective mechanisms that are flexible. She further advises that instead of becoming fixated with coming up with an ideal, we get used to coming up with models and learning to adjust them when circumstances change. "Democracy was designed to change with times," says Mark, a recent retiree from the United States. In the democratic context, equality might begin from the premise of drafting a set of values that are important in a democratic society today. This premise would be informed by the understanding that equality does not lead to freedom and that freedom does not meet equality by design. The two are different, but they are not the opposite. They are compatible, and they are part of a sequence. These ideas echo across conversations, including one with Olga, from Greece, who talks about democracy emanating from "a shared sense of culture." We begin by figuring out what is valuable in a democratic society and plan how to safeguard access to that, through a draft, which becomes a model that then evolves to a mechanism that adjusts as our needs evolve, change, or demand.

Voice

Speaking one's mind on equal terms is an indisputable attribute of democracy. For citizens of authoritarian or semi-authoritarian states, this point of discussion conjures up painful memories, as it does for those who have fled dictatorial regimes or spent some of their adult lives in societies that restricted their ability to speak. As voice emerges as a consistent theme throughout my interviews, the stories I listen to diverge and reflect individual experiences. Nikos, from Greece, speaks with me about the ethos of democracy and the democratic birthright: the right to speak and be heard among equals. I am simultaneously inspired and perplexed by the power of these words. The right to speak and be heard should be a given, and to do so responsibly is what makes us human. The equality question confuses me, not for lack of conviction in the merit of equality but for the lack of a consistent and shared definition of what equality means. Greece is a country that has experienced occupation, followed by civil war, followed by civil unrest, followed by a military coup d'état, followed by free elections, all within the course of thirty years. Recently, it elected the most leftist party it has ever had into government, only to see it formulate an alliance with the most extreme right-wing party so as to attain the parliamentary majority required to form a government. The Greek bailout referendum in 2015 asked Greek citizens whether they wanted to stay in the European Union and accept its strict economic policies for reform within the Eurozone, or to leave. The binary referendum choice further polarized the country. A majority voted in favor of leaving the European Union, much like their fellow E.U. constituents in the United Kingdom did a year later. Regardless, Greece ended up staying in the European Union. Greeks are sarcastic these days about the circumstances around which their referendum vote was reversed and offer the following, unsolicited advice on Brexit: "If you would like to find out how a referendum vote is reversed, come talk to Prime Minister Tsipras."

Talk about voice, equality, and freedom with my respondents has a way of marrying tragedy, sarcasm, poignancy, and hope in unexpected ways that seek to normalize experiences that are diverse, traumatizing, and disillusioning. My conversations in Russia frequently reference the restrictions of the Stalinist era, the hope and civil unrest that perestroika ushered in, the excess of civil unrest, the growth of the mafia, and the constant irreverence that characterized the Yeltsin era. What the rest of the world reads as white or black is a persistent gray area for Russians. Putin has polarized Russia, many Russians find, drawing it further away from some of its potential European allies. Yet, at the same time, he has put an end to the state of anarchy that rendered public safety obsolete during the Yeltsin era. No one disputes the absolutist affect that characterizes Putin's political approach to national and global diplomacy. Yet, at the same time, many Russians wonder whether in Western democracies we receive the same restricted set of choices, dressed differently as democratically curated options.

Voice is key for people who have grown up in Russia during these years, and the conversations I have are filled with nuance. Viktor and Simela, both in their late fifties, both heads of families that have gone through several career shifts due to regime changes in Russia, emphasize the importance of having the right to think and speak freely. Pavlos and Ekaterina, younger, hopeful and cynical at the same time, are measured. Pavlos tells me that "democracy is [a] wonderful thing with grand theories, but people are not grand enough to make it work." Ekaterina looks me in the eye and tells me firmly that we have the right to speak, yes, but we also have the obligation to protect a democratic society. Valeria, the photojournalist flaneuse, firmly tells me that voice in a democracy is the responsibility of the state but is also the responsibility of the citizen. I point out that this sounds like John F. Kennedy's famous line asking not just what your country can do for you but what you can do for your country. She explains that voice is both a right to be protected by the government and something that people must put to work.

The emphasis on the responsibility of citizens to do this work resurfaces in conversations I have in China. The importance of voice is a given, but people speak in careful and clear terms about how this right is to be savored and not squandered. All of my respondents acknowledge the monitorial practices of their government. It is difficult to find a government that does not engage in monitorial activity. Surveillance is and perhaps always has been an aspect of governance. The platforms used to surveil make these practices more visible to, intrusive for, and felt by citizens. In acknowledging this, Cheer, a programmer for a large technology company, talks with me in a deeply moving way about the personal responsibility of citizens to protect their right to voice. Jack, an undergraduate student studying economics, has trouble blaming others for ways in which his right to speak may be negated. There is a reluctance to shift the blame onto others for the wrongs of the state. Even Gary, a tour guide and the most cynical and critical of my respondents, is affable and effortlessly immediate: "What democracy? We don't have democracy!" he exclaims, as we walk past some trees that are five hundred years old. Yet when talking about the right to speak, he is adamant that it is his responsibility to fight for it, to protect it, and to ensure that others, including his newly born son, get to enjoy it.

It is to be expected that the right to voice is not taken for granted by people living under regimes that have semi-authoritarian forms of rule. I notice the same urgency about protecting the right to voice when I speak with refugees. The right to voice is prized as the holy grail of democracy.

The more marginalized people feel, the more urgent the need to speak. Hamid, from Ghana, associates voice with wanting "to say your best, do your best, having the right to aspire." Uzma, from Pakistan, tells me that freedom of speech is important, but "people must know the rules, must be educated" about that which they speak. And then I talk with Golab, who fled the Taliban in Afghanistan, and he tells me, in pitch-perfect and slightly British-accented English, "We all want to be heard, but we must learn to listen to each other."

Who needs theory to interpret these responses, when the words of the people reflect the insights of philosophical thought with such clarity and immediacy? The gravitas of these testimonials on the importance of voice sits with me as, once back in the United States, I converse with those who struggle with democracy and voice in a different context. When people talk about voice, they talk primarily about the right to vote. "People have a voice: people have a vote!" blurts out Monica, a vivacious woman in her early sixties who dislikes the "stay-at-home mom" label, and so together we ascribe the title of "home engineer and project manager." Yes, we have an equal voice, "in theory," says Mark. But people don't dodge responsibility for lack of voice here either. They just express dissatisfaction in a different manner. My respondents talk about the importance of having a say in the rules of governance. They speak thoughtfully about observing democratic principles in political governance, in how corporations are run, and in how families work together. Their political affiliations are brought up casually as the conversation progresses, and they range from the extreme right to the extreme left. The one thing in common is respecting the will of the majority and the right to vote. "I voted so I could complain," quips Sara, a vibrant bartender. She quickly adds, "If you did not vote, you have no right to complain when things go wrong."

It is clear that voice is important to all and a core construct of democracy. And perhaps we have more access to voice and participation than we did in the past, as Annett, a German retired retailer in her mid-eighties, reminds me. What emerges is that voice means different things to people. Some equate it with the right to vote, while others talk more broadly about the civic responsibility to speak up.

Discontent about speaking and not being heard emerges when I talk with people about the problems of democracy. For the time being, in locating voice at the heart of democracy, I am reminded of the words of the political scientist Stephen Coleman, who in surveying U.K. politics remarked that people are increasingly being counted but not feeling counted.[40] What is voice? More than simply speaking.

Skepticism

After discussing people's answers to my questions about democracy, some ask me, "Did I get it right?" I explain that there is no right or wrong answer. Once they begin to talk with me about equality and voice as the core pillars of democracy, an inescapable and deeply rooted skepticism emerges. "We the people," scoffs Sara. "No one wants to be equal and free. Everyone just wants to be better."

On the same note, "What good is a democracy if it offers no way for me to improve my circumstances?" Gary jokes with me in Beijing. This is not a selfish statement; it is a cynical statement, rooted in the belief that democracy is not a system of governance but a way of living together that affords all equal access to opportunity. It is a definition that is common, but it is one that connects democracy to the economy more than we realize or are willing to admit. As I follow the spiral of skepticism around the world, I get to listen to similar opinions, in different languages, with different words, and in different accents. Estella, from Canada, drops the following words as I ask her what comes to mind when she hears the word "democracy": "Collective, consensus, and limited choices." She explains that "there is an ideal of choice, but it really is distilled to a set of limited options." Khrilid, a refugee from Morocco, points out that people want more choice but often have to choose the option that is the least worst. " 'Democracy' is a word that is easily manipulated, to serve different purposes"—these are the first words I hear from Drew, from the United States. Hamid, in talking about both his home country of Ghana and Greece, where he finds himself in refugee status, tells me frankly that there is no democracy anywhere, then exclaims, "It is more like anarchy!" "What is democracy?" I ask Marya, in the United States: "*Not* Trump," she quips.

These remarks are accompanied by eye rolls, sly smiles, and sighs. People laugh out of exasperation. They try to be thoughtful and in the process find themselves becoming cynical. This is not surprising. Cynicism is a defining characteristic of contemporary citizenship. It is augmented by polling processes. It is further ampli-fied by the generic mechanisms that politicians use to talk at but not with publics. It is enhanced by the way politicians and media restrict voice by listening to it only selectively. Finally, it is something that comes with experience, with knowledge, and with history. People who have lived, seen, observed, and learned will be skeptical. We lose our civic naiveté as we become civic adults. Skepticism is the price we pay for experience and knowledge. I am not sure anyone can go through hardship and not emerge skeptically. Skepticism is a badge we should wear with pride. Cynicism carries a bitterness that often leads to the loss of civic hope. It is one thing no longer to be naive; it is an entirely different thing to be hopeless. I am not wor-ried about the skepticism that my conversational companions dem-onstrate. I am drawn to it and admire it. I am afraid of cynicism because it implies surrender. Skepticism is a healthy reaction to problems that have no easy solutions.

Coming up with a definition of democracy that lasts forever is an impossible problem. Democracy is a fixed ideal with flexible mor-phology, one that must be adjusted with the least measure of com-promise. How do we come up with a definition that lasts forever? With a definition that is always modern? What makes things mod-ern? Why do we recognize them as modern even after several years (or centuries) have passed since their inception? It is their ability to convey the moment, now and forever, to transmit the feeling of what it means to be of the moment. We can never be consistently modern. We remember and reimagine our past to situate the present, and then we map the present to consider the future. Sure, we live in the ephemera of the modern, but those are and must be, by definition, moments. This is not a bad thing. Modern is the now; off-modern is the imagined. Narratives of the off-modern open the modernity of the *what-if*.[41] A mix of nostalgia and aspira-tion lies beneath our collective imaginings of what might be. As we look for the ideal, we are unwittingly romanced by the trappings of the past. We look at the future with the feeling that there was something better that preceded it, something that was somehow lost.

And so we pause for thought when asked the question of democracy. We are ambivalent, and we are skeptical. We latch onto our familiar vocabulary of voice and equality—not because we do not understand, at heart, what democracy is about but possibly because we lack a modern vocabulary with which to describe it, and this would be the starting point for change.

THREE

To Be a Citizen

What does it mean to be a citizen? This is the second question my conversation companions and I consider together. The question prompts a consideration of what constitutes good citizenship. If the themes of the previous chapter coalesced around ideas of voice and equality, the themes that prevail in this chapter portray a noble citizen who is often rendered invisible in the process of governance. The question of citizenship, much like the question of democracy, has perplexed people for centuries. Nobility and invisibility have often defined our conversations about citizenship. Aristotle, the philosopher who wrote about the notion *areté*, the ideal of a happy and virtuous life, was also the one to connect this life to civic practices and duties. Yet in *Politics*, he had confessed to a general inability to come up with a concise definition of citizenship, specifically because the question of citizenship, much like the question of democracy, is often disputed.[1] In place of definition, we identify practices that evoke in us a sense of civic fulfillment. *Areté*, a Greek word that reflects what we now commonly understand as well-being, was dependent, for Aristotle, on our civic duty. For Aristotle, the civic condition, much like the democratic condition, was above all a human condition. Being a good citizen was the way to becoming a better human. Looking after the common good as a way of living our lives paved the way for good citizenship, democracy, and what might be understood as a virtuous and fulfilling life. While our thinking on the question of citizenship has become more nuanced and evolved beyond the Aristotelian times of inequality and slavery, the ideal of the good citizen striving for the virtuous life is the constant that has defined both how we study and how we speak about citizenship.

For the ancient Greeks, citizenship was connected to living a virtuous life in service of democracy. This was understood to be a complex task, involving pragmatic and moral conflict. Still, it reflects an ethos of being, which came to attain legal ties to the state during the Greco-Roman period. During Roman times, civil ties to the state were explicitly laid out, and that is where we start to see the roots of the thinking that situates the citizen as a subject of the state. An understanding of civil citizenship, cemented during that era, evolved to specify that all citizens hold equal rights and are equally accountable before the law. This is conditional equality, of course, as these rights typically exclude women, people of color, non-property owners, and various nomadic groups that choose to exist beyond the perimeter of the state. It was around the same time that citizenship began to connect loosely to a particular geolocality, and this tendency prevailed as nation-states began to form and attain stability. It is striking to hear the qualities of virtue, equality before the law, and equality of rights persist throughout the ages and emerge in the responses I receive to the question of citizenship.

For the majority of those I've interviewed residing in the United States and Germany, the first response to the question of citizenship has to do with being a citizen of their country. "It is your birthright, your nationality," says one person, while another one adds, "It has to do with where you were born and the responsibilities that come with being part of this country." While most recognize that "citizenship begins with your passport but goes beyond that," few can give me responses that deviate from the way they identify nationally. This is not surprising or uncommon. If citizenship has to do with respect for the common rule, it is reasonable to have a nation-state be the first reference point that people evoke.

In so doing, people reflect practices that they have been civically socialized to adopt. Historically, we have observed three models of citizenship, in the following order: civil to political to social.[2] Civil aspects of citizenship involve equal standards regarding how the law is applied. Political aspects of citizenship primarily revolve around voting obligations. Social aspects of citizenship reflect community-oriented activities pursued by members of a society, to ensure that all are treated fairly and that the social welfare of all is secured. Participant responses cover all three aspects of citizenship, although the order in which they are addressed varies, depending on cultural background.

People I've interviewed from Russia and China, for example, speak first about the notion of social responsibility. Ekaterina, a young nutritionist, tells me that to be a citizen means first to acknowledge your social rights and social obligations. Viktor, who first trained to be a lawyer pre-perestroika and then became a prison warder post-perestroika and presently is the chief supervisor for one of Russia's largest airports, talks to me about family being at the center of good citizenship. To be a citizen means to raise your children well so they will contribute to society. Valeria, born in Belarus and presently living in St. Petersburg, begins to respond by telling me a story: "When I worked as a journalist, I spent time interviewing people in disadvantaged neighborhoods. I realized these people had simple dreams, and they had to with getting through the day and doing their work perfectly. And in doing so, they also looked after their community. For me, this is a good citizen." In Beijing, Jack talks to me about how being a citizen has to do with caring for others. Gary emphasizes the importance of being able to care for his family.

By contrast, responses to the question of citizenship in the United States are driven by civil responsibility and often note the need to abide by the common rules, applying the same civil rights to all, ensuring that everyone follows the rule of law. The civil aspect comes first, as responses overwhelmingly begin with phrases that include respecting the laws of the country, defending the Constitution, respecting the freedoms that come with being a citizen of the United States, abiding by the rules, and adhering to the rules of governance. Immediately following these responses, which are often presented as a proviso, people shift to political responsibilities and speak about voting as a civic obligation, as something that must be done. The importance of voting is emphasized equally among all my informants, to the point that I start worrying that I am only speaking to those who vote, who, incidentally, made up barely over 50 percent of the country's population in the 2016 presidential election. I remind myself that the nature of my work and the questions I ask are the aspiration, so often the responses I receive are about what people would like to do, rather than what they often opt to do, for a variety of reasons. This book is about what we might like democracy to be, not what it is like.

Conversations with people in the United States also focus on contributing to a community, and they speak about this with the same passion that their fellow citizens in Russia and China display. So I begin to document how much our cultural process of socialization influences how we prioritize our obligations as citizens and how it defines the vocabulary we fall back on, like a safety blanket, when we are asked to free-associate about what it means to be a citizen. In Germany, a sense of citizenship is often associated with state membership, state-granted rights and obligations. Still, several of my German respondents speak of a need for cultural assimilation, in a way that invites respecting others' cultural conventions within Ger-

many but also when traveling beyond it. Even though all participants connect the right to citizenship to the state, the sense of a
commonly shared set of cultural values permeates all responses. The
same spirit resurfaces in a different manner in the United Kingdom,
possibly in reaction to recent political developments. Citizenship is
"respect for democratic values, irrespective of your country of resi-
dence," says Thomas, an information-technology worker from the
United Kingdom.

In Mexico and Brazil, I am met with a mix of pragmatism and
philosophy. People often skip over giving me a definition and directly tell me what is wrong with things. I enjoy this conversational
rule-breaking because reimagining something requires breaking
with convention. Louis from Mexico City embarks on a passionate
analysis of how citizens are restricted by the system, and I follow
along as we converse in English and Spanish. Kristi, who grew up in
Ecuador, studied in the United States and Italy, and presently re-
sides in Greece, had told me the same thing when we spoke in
Greece: "It [is] the participatory framework that constrains us."
Myrna briefly answers my question, but I can tell she is more interested in talking about citizen apathy in Mexico and what lies behind
it. Daniela, a well-known TV anchor, leans across the table and
talks with me about what we can do together to change things. In
Brazil, Patrícia courteously answers my question quickly before she
moves on to what really interests her: "Being a citizen means being
fully aware and committed to someone's role in a society, to exercise
critical thinking, to have a positive attitude, and to help the ones in
need." Cinthia openly talks about all the things that present thorny
topics of conversations in the United States, as she draws a precise
distinction between rights and duties: "Citizens' rights include
health care, education, housing, safety, access to work and food,
public transportation, free association, religious freedom, and the
right to peacefully protest. Duties include observing the laws, respecting the rights of all, caring for and protecting children and the

incapacitated, preserving nature, voting, and other duties as provided by the Constitution." I visited both countries in the middle of
pre-election politics, and conversations everywhere revolve around
corruption. But corruption does not have geographic specificity; it
exists everywhere. What fascinates me the most is how the habits,
the language, and civic instincts fluctuate.

Coffee-shop philosophy is the national pastime in my native
country of Greece, so responses there range from understanding
what having a civic consciousness means to deep analyses of Greeks
as not anarchists but *anarchoi*—which generally refers not to disre-
specting order but rather to not having an interest in a sense of
order. The responses I receive around the world mix convention
with folklore and personality in a way that energizes conversation
and still manages to leave the main question unanswered. *What is
citizenship?* It appears to relate to a broad range of things that are
responses that we have been conditioned to provide, based on
where and how we grew up. It also appears to be challenged by a
distaste for the conventions that have rendered us into civic beings.

Commonalities develop around how systems of governance are
organized and oriented toward citizens. In theory, we typically distinguish between a civic republican model and a more liberally oriented one that followed the former, during the various waves of
democratic evolution.[3] The civic republican model rests on ideas of
civic virtue and is directed toward the pursuit of virtuous community
life. It emanates from the premise that all citizens are equally motivated for *areté* but also assumes that the state will be just and mag-
nanimous in its ruling, although how this will occur is not strictly
defined. The alternative and more liberal model addresses this nebu-
lous area to define exactly how the state will be able to afford equal
opportunity. Through turmoil and the various revolutions that followed the Middle Ages, citizens have negotiated a liberal model that
asks the state to take specific steps to ensure that all citizens enjoy
equal rights freely. Both models present an enlightened path to citi-

zenship, but they differ in the form of support provided to citizens through state governance. My conversations with people reconcile the republican and the liberal model but come to an impasse when state governance is involved. There seems to be a general reluctance to involve the state, despite the assumption that it is the state that has set the rules, the boundaries, and the civic territory that citizens must follow. People are keen to remind me of all the responsibilities that citizens have, including the need to protect the responsibilities of others, and nowhere in the conversation does the state come up as a factor. Interestingly enough, the state remains an invisible actor as conversations travel from semi-authoritarian states to seemingly liberal states to troubled democracies.

There are obscure references to politicians on occasion, and there are abstract nods to being restricted, although rarely do folks name the parties responsible. When it comes to the question of responsibility, the citizen is responsible for a number of things, including being educated; being informed about everything; being an engaged community member; voting on everything, even the most minuscule things; expressing opinions but not ones that trespass on the rights of others; getting people to homeless shelters; looking after the community; and countless other tasks including having a job, paying taxes, and raising a civically involved family. This seems like a busy day for the everyday citizen, especially in regimes where access to education and information is not easy. I think of the ancient times, when being a citizen did not involve work, for that was perceived as distracting people from an active and virtuous life in the polity. Work was delegated to slaves, who did not have a voice and took on the burden of working so that others could speak. Still, in theory and in practice, when people talk about citizenship, they talk about a lot of work that needs to be done, and they rarely discuss the merits of citizenship.

Political thought follows this trail. Historically, citizenship emerged more prominently in the sixteenth century, when it was revisited as a way of reinforcing sovereignty and stability for emerging nation-states. Subjects became citizens as monarchs granted specific rights to advance the priorities of their nation-state. The concept of citizenship is flexible, but not to the advantage of the individual. Citizenship bends and adjusts to support evolving regimes of socioeconomic power. John Locke connected the notion of civility to the rights to life, freedom, and private property. Jean-Jacques Rousseau's ideas evolved to speak specifically to the principles and merits of civic association, with fraternity at the center of the social contract that binds citizens but more important commits the state to certain obligations. This core idea plants the seeds for a more liberally oriented model of civic engagement and governance. As that model meets the forces of puritanism, capitalism, industrialization, and revolutions, rights are negotiated, but a foundational model of engagement that defines citizenship remains beyond our reach. It is easier for us to use the concept to describe patterns of exclusion, inclusion, power struggles, inequalities, and social injustice than it is to define. Perhaps it is more useful to do so, as citizenship bends and adjusts, depending on the context. Yet this leaves citizens with one option only when looking for paths to good citizenship, and it revolves around engagement that promotes civic virtue. As this noble citizen emerges as the core theme that unites all the stories my informants share with me, I can't help but think, Where is the noble state?

The Noble Citizen

I think of citizenship as laying out the contours of the map we use to navigate democracy.[4] My own understanding of citizenship is fluid and deeply contextual. Although there are common threads that connect civic practices to public affairs and political engagement, the civic habits that define what it means to be a citizen evolve and vary, temporally and geographically. We are confined, guided, and empowered by historical and cultural context, as we carve a path to citizenship that combines private and public practices. If citizenship maps out the civic path we follow, technology is what we use to imagine, construct, and redraft this map. Some technology stays the same, and certain aspects of technology evolve; but whether it is the alphabet, the practice of writing, the ability to publish broadly, the use of tools to share oral stories and histories, the ability to travel, the opportunity to listen to, watch, and experience worlds beyond our reach, or the capacity to speak and potentially be heard, the technology of any given era will inevitably be connected to how we practice citizenship. Maps are drawn, after all, so that we can connect pathways and so that we understand what it takes to be connected. Technology, in its many iterations, has provided the media, the conduits, for civic connection.

As I speak with people across the world, it becomes clear that citizenship rests on gestures of connection, cooperation, and conversation that evolve as citizens become involved and disillusioned by the rhythms and rituals of democracy. What does it ultimately mean to be a democratic person?[5] It is clear from my conversations that the more politicians withdraw from direct contact with the electorate, the less interested the public becomes. Citizens have strong ideas, but my conversations reveal that they have grown tired of talking and not being heard.

The first theme that connects my conversations is an aspirational model that I refer to as that of the noble citizen. People recognize the core elements of a meaningful civic life, one that allows them to get ahead while also helping others in need. Nobody harbors any illusions that this is an ideal we have ever come close to attaining, individually or collaboratively. We have always functioned within the nexus of a long and imperfect, ever evolving path to citizenship. Democracy evolves, and citizenship is adjusted to the times; but the connection between the two remains.

"What is citizenship?" I ask. A colorful array of responses emerges. "To be a well-rounded member of a democratic society," says Mark, a micro-brewer in his early thirties from Illinois. It is about contributing, abiding by the rules, and having respect for these agreed-on rules. It is about "respect for the environment, respect for the work of others, respect for a set of common values," adds Efi, a hairstylist from Greece in her mid-twenties. To exercise citizenship is to "be fully aware and committed to someone's role in a society, to exercise critical thinking, to have a positive attitude, and to help the ones in need," says Patrícia from Brazil, in the gentle, calm tone one attains as a midlife adult. "You want to aspire. You want to give your best," adds Hamid, passionately and in a rushed tone, as if we are going to run out of time and this is his last chance to get these things out of his mind and onto my recorder. Being a citizen implies a social, civic, and political responsibility, says Myrna, a journalist based in Mexico City. Citizens "should be interested in everyday events in the country, read the newspapers, participate in the political debates, and demand to governing authorities to do their job," she adds. "Beyond vote and recycle," Anna from Canada tells me. "My duty is to speak back to the government if they are not doing well, through whatever means, not just voting but participation of all kinds," she affirms.

Myrna continues to distinguish what people feel they ought to do and what they feel compelled to do. She explains that corruption, fraud, and government inaction often discourage citizens to take action, confining them to positions that are often misread as apathy. There are frequent pauses in my conversation with people on the topic of citizenship, and they are reflective of the long distance between what people want to do, what they can do, and whether what they will do is worth doing. Aspirational skepticism drives these responses that always center around this ideal of noble citizenship.

It is in this context that those I meet discuss problems associated with representation, literacy, transparency, and communication. These so-called global citizens are most often of mixed origins. I may locate them in Russia, but they identify as part Russian and part Belarussian or Uzbekistani. I may encounter them in Greece, but they have fled from Syria. I may meet with them in the United Kingdom, but they were raised in Saudi Arabia. "Canadians are frequently portrayed as ideal citizens, . . . with many assuming that this is a liberal Trudeauian utopia, but there is a lot of control and discrimination here too, perhaps not as extreme as in other places, but it still exists," says Estella. The people I speak with express an acute interest in being good citizens, but they also seem frustrated at the lack of avenues they may follow in doing so. Several speak of a lack of *representative equality*. Beyond ideological representation, citizens are concerned that racial, ethnic, gender, and class representations in elected governance privilege elites and neglect the interests of the masses.

These concerns are not new. Citizens have always had to live with the burden that they are doing a lot and that yet somehow that is not enough. A long history of imperfect citizenship casts a shadow on the earnest aspirations of contemporary generations. It communicates an abstract ideal of virtue. Rousseau complained, "We have physicists, geometers, chemists, astronomers, poets, musicians, and painters; we no longer have citizens."[6] Rarely do we consider how the professional sphere displaces activities of a civic nature. One might wonder about the role of corporations, for instance, and how often they benefit from a certain national affiliation or a lack thereof. Permissive laws in the United States for technology companies contradict more defined legal frameworks that exist in the European Union, for instance. In such cases, corporations benefit from the legal framework of one country yet show no allegiance to a specific country when it comes to profit incentives that include sharing data on citizens in ways that influence our infoscape. Many people question the incompatibility of material culture with the virtuous aspirations expected of citizens. Despite an admiration for the American model of democratic equality, Alexis de Tocqueville was deeply concerned about the ability to reconcile material security with civic virtue.[7] John Dewey was hopeful about the role that communication and journalism might play in enabling good citizens, yet the quality of the information provided by contemporary media is identified by many informants as a primary obstacle to the citizenship path.[8] Walter Lippmann worried that individual members of a society would be much too self-centered to cater to the needs of the whole.[9] The people I have met while doing research for this book aspire to evolve beyond the locus of the self and to contribute, but the texture of their voice reveals ambivalence in their ability to achieve those aspirations. The sociologist Charles Wright Mills predicted that mass representative democracies might prescribe channels of participation so narrow that citizens might quickly feel restrained and eventually become "strangers to politics."[10] Citizenship bends and adjusts, yes, but is it flexible to the point where it has become spineless?

I admire the civic fervor that drives my respondents as they passionately speak about the need to move beyond the beaten path, the need to be more engaged. I worry that they work long hours, bear countless responsibilities, face injustice, and seek to overcome it, and yet, when seeking to be more civically involved, the primary avenue of doing so is a referendum designed to support a political argument or an election that involves compromising on the least objectionable candidate. Debbie, a youthful personal trainer, speaks fervently about how "your vote is your voice, and your voice is your power." She talks about participation that is focused on protecting the marginalized and making a change, concluding, "This is not a spectator sport; this is about participation." It takes me a moment to digest this powerful statement, for several reasons. First, I am impressed by the courage behind it. Second, I worry that systems of governance offer few ways in which civic engagement can be anything but a spectator sport.

In mapping out "the lonely crowd," the sociologist David Riesman and his colleagues sketched out how middle-class Americans have become increasingly trapped in post-industrial avenues of engagement that invite spectatorship and indifference, giving responses that might frequently fall under the "don't know" polling category.[11] It is this tendency that most of my respondents are fighting against, but my concern is that we no longer provide ways for them to be seen. The lonely crowd has morphed into lonely citizens, as the trends that Riesman and his colleagues identify have evolved along with our technologies. Lonely citizens are frequently forced to choose between yes and no, to approve or disapprove polling options; refusing to do so or selecting anything in between renders them invisible.

The Invisible Citizen

Edward R. Murrow once remarked that "just because your voice now goes all across the world does not mean you are any wiser than when it only went to the end of the bar."[12] I study how technology impacts democracy and politics, so I use this quotation often to explain how media amplify our voices but do not necessarily make us more knowledgeable or audible.

Media create an illusion of visibility. By design, a platform like Twitter allows us to say something that is potentially accessible to everyone. But who is "everyone"? We are heard but only by those who have access to the internet and Twitter, who happen to tune in at that time, who have algorithmic profiles that prioritize our posts, and who are generally predisposed to be interested in what we have to say. Our voice online is made stronger by our network of followers, who may choose to elevate what we say to prominence, nullify it, or simply ignore it. We often claim that the voice is amplified. Sure, we give people a megaphone with a wide reach. Does this make us more audible? For how long? If we reach more people, does this mean that those are the people who can effect change? It is important to have a voice, yes, but it is not enough. It is even more significant for that voice to be loud, to have an impact, and to be listened to. Citizens' voice is a core element of democracy, but on its own, it does not enable paths to good citizenship.

So far, in connecting themes of participation that people bring up when talking about citizenship, I have been retelling and weaving their stories together. I rely on what people tell me, and I try to figure out what sort of civic map it suggests. I am keenly aware, however, that there are a lot of things people will not tell me, for a number of reasons. First, despite my efforts to establish rapport with them, I am a stranger who has crossed their path. Second, I ask questions that people have both an easy and a hard time being honest about. It is easy to admit that one is let down by democracy. It is difficult to describe what one might do. It is not socially desirable to confess to not being a good citizen. Finally, it is impossible to know whether one is a good or bad citizen in the absence of a universally accepted model of what being a citizen means.

I am sure that my conversational companions are earnest about being involved and sincere in their efforts to be better. I am worried that they do not have paths to do more and be better. And I am further concerned that civic paths to enlightened citizenship are becoming blocked, complicated, and congested, even though technology promises to make these paths more accessible. So, ultimately, there are things my informants will not tell me because they have not thought of them. There are aspects of citizenship that have not occurred to them, civic ways of thinking that they have not been socialized into, practices that are not formally validated or recognized, tiny acts of civic participation that we conduct every day that do not count and are not seen. And because they are not seen, they are forgotten by all, even by their instigators, us.

So let me write now about the things that people do not talk about and how, by not talking about them, they render those things, and themselves, unseen, uncounted, unheard. As citizens, we often move within the civic parameters delineated in a world that has taught us to see, and pay attention to, outliers. We are gradually conditioned to notice that which is loud, provocative, out of the ordinary. Our media culture is structured on an attention economy

that further reinforces and reproduces the unusual. We never learn to listen to the ordinary. We never focus on the value of the average. We gloss over the ordinary, consistent acts of daily civic participation to highlight the heroic, the messianic, and the extraordinary. We thus learn that we must move beyond the beaten path so that we can be seen. In a world saturated with information, it is often the sensational that is elevated to prominence, and this is a trend that the media, politicians, and several of us have learned to game.[13]

The noble citizen thus is destined to become, unfortunately and inadvertently, an invisible citizen to the state, a citizen who is not recognized for one's efforts and contributions, a citizen addressed from a variety of platforms, digital and non-, but a citizen rarely seen for who one actually is. And yet this noble citizen is who people aspire to be, in their earnest responses to me. The ordinary citizens are unseen.

The sociologist and political scientist Richard Sennett has written of this invisibility before. He made the argument that as media increasingly commercialized public spaces for conversation, ordinary citizens found themselves shut out of meaningful paths to participation in public affairs. He called this gradual retreat from the public to the private sphere "the fall of public man."[14] The greater argument here was that it was not just a loss of public space for deliberation to be lamented but also a plurality of conversation that these spaces supported. Sennett, as well as his mentor, the renowned Hannah Arendt, understood plurality as the core value of democratic deliberation. The growing commercialization of public spaces advanced against the cultivation of public spaces for conversation. To fully appreciate this, one must understand that conversations about public affairs thrive in casual interactions and accidental circumstances. Rarely do people sit down for the explicit purpose of having a conversation about politics, and when they do, they are possibly not enjoying it all that much. Typically, we talk about politics in the midst of many other pastimes and obligations, and that is

what is both appropriate and fascinating. Politics coexist with our everyday routines, and they find their way into our sometimes mundane everyday conversational routines. Think about the casual political comment that you exchange every once in a while with your neighbor as you both take your dogs out for a walk. Consider the occasional brief interlude about politics and the meaning of life that you might have with the corner deli cashier. For those of you who live in cities, ruminate on slow walks you might take and brief conversations you strike up with familiar strangers. I do not suggest that these conversations are no longer possible. We are humans, and we are social and political by nature. As long as we exist, we will have these conversations. But as our walks through parks become more rushed because our work schedules are more defined and must align with global time zones, as our interactions in the cashier line become more formulaic because they conform to the organizational logic of convenience and expedience, we find less inspiration to talk about these things, as we stand in line at Starbucks, Whole Foods, Costco, or any other massively produced and consumed chain. Simultaneously, we are hard-pressed to find the time to keep up with the news of the day, so we often use that time to catch up with what our friends are doing or read about current events on our mobile phones, only to then be potentially accused of antisocially spending too much time on the screen.

Therefore, we are restricted, both geographically and temporally. We have fewer spaces and less time to spend on public affairs. Sennett further made the point that this fusion of "public geography and capitalism" resulted in synchronous "withdrawal from the public into the family" and "confusion about the materials of public appearance, a confusion which could be turned into a profit."[15] The commercialization of public spaces not only dislocates public activity but also creates a paradox for the modern individual who is offered public spaces that possess *visibility* but do not enable *collectivity*. It is this sentiment of personal isolation in the midst of ultimate public visibility that captures the political mood of contemporary citizens who are suspended in these public spaces with the absence of what Arendt terms the "in-between," that is, "the specific and usually irreplaceable in-between which should have been formed between the individual and his fellow men."[16] My informants do not speak about the conditions that preceded the loss of the in-between bond, because they are too involved in resurrecting these bonds and in striving to be noble citizens despite the temporal and spatial confines they face. Still, these impediments persist and potentially compromise the impact of our civic activity.

For example, as we retreat from public spaces to the privacy of our phones and look for spaces there where we may read, connect, and express ourselves, we find ourselves interacting with others in online spaces that promise visibility but are not designed to promote collectivity or collaboration. Platforms like Twitter, for instance, thrive because they meet both our diminished access to time and our need for public space. They promise public space, globally visible, and require a minimal time commitment: what we can muster in 280 characters. Granted, we often become involved in conversations online that become more time-consuming than this initial premise. We may still use these platforms to engage in collective action to connect and mobilize around important issues. We will also use them to engage in sometimes meaningful and often toxic arguments. Of course, we have a choice in how we use them. We are masters of our own fate. However, increasingly our ability to choose becomes restricted. So instead of choosing between appealing options, we are offered narrowly defined and precurated feeds to choose from, and our opinions are further algorithmically crunched into these narratives that promise visibility but do not ensure that we will be seen.[17] These feeds simultaneously publicize and oppress viewpoints, to the beat of an attention economy.[18] Estimates, often inaccurate, of what will potentially capture the broad attention drive the production of conversational feeds that give form to these online spaces. And yet these spaces are nothing without our voices to populate them. They are rendered into being through our connections, networks, and conversations. In the end, we are given a voice but with no guarantee that we will be listened to. It is one thing to be visible; it a very different thing to be seen for who one is. It is one thing to speak; it is another thing to be listened to, and it is yet a different thing to be understood and appreciated.

Yet what citizens want to do at heart is to participate, observe, and become involved. The political scientist Michael Schudson described this aptly as the form of a "monitorial citizen." In his influential book *The Good Citizen*, Schudson went after critics of contemporary democracies that rushed to judge modern citizens as passive, apathetic, and disinterested. On the contrary, his historical analysis revealed that citizens had never been recognized as being particularly involved. Importantly, the assumption that a civic era of enlightened and engaged citizenship preceded ours was a fiction. Our civic ancestors were about as apathetic as we might be or, viewed differently, were no less politically motivated than we are. Evidence showed that we have always been considered mediocre citizens by the critical minds of each era. Either we have always failed at being good citizens, or we have set the bar too high.

Schudson then went on to explain that being an active citizen committed to serving the common good was perhaps not as effortless a task as we may have assumed. The pressures of everyday life, including procuring for one's family and struggling with illness, hardship, and war, often prevented preceding generations from tending to their civic duties. While many of those pressures were alleviated through the progress of medicine, science, and automation, the new industrial and post-industrial routines were often incompatible with the deliberative practices that democracy requires. Reading, reflection, conversation, disagreement, and reconciliation are all deliberative processes that take time, occur spontaneously, often evolve inefficiently, and run counter to the precision and schedules of newly introduced post-industrial routines. Whereas citizens of prior eras often lacked equal access to education, information, and participation, those of recent ones have enjoyed higher levels of literacy, greater knowledge of public affairs, and increased access. Still, the paths to democratic participation have grown both more accessible and more complex to navigate. While media has afforded wide access to information that assists citizens in the deliberation of important issues of the day, the sheer amount of information available, the number of issues to confront, and the scale of democracy in mass societies appear daunting. The increased work hours have left little time for people to traverse a political landscape saturated with information and overpopulated with representatives, issues, and decisions to be made. Schudson suggested that the millennial citizen was not apathetic but perhaps more comfortable in monitorial mode. He understood this citizen as "defensive rather than proactive," describing an individual who "is not an absentee citizen but watchful, even while he or she is doing something else."[19]

There is a form of cognitive and emotional multitasking embedded in the complex webs of information overload that monitorial citizens manage. These connect to the greater question of temporal and geographical constraints we face as we go through our daily civic routines. My conversational companions do not speak about this multitasking, but I observe it at work during our conversations. Mobile phones are always nearby and frequently checked. Walks in public spaces tend to invite thoughtful, relaxed, and lengthier conversations. Meetings in chain-operated cafés result in shorter conversations, as do those scheduled on breaks from work. Schudson's monitorial citizens understand civic duty as a predominantly monitorial obligation, stemming from the necessity to remain informed to be able to contribute intelligently in public administration, mostly in the event of a crisis. They "scan (rather than read) the informational environment . . . so that they may be alerted on a variety of issues . . . and may be mobilized around those issues in a large variety of ways."[20] The monitorial modality is frequently referenced in my conversations, as my informants regularly bring up the need to stay informed and be educated about public affairs. They also bring up the difficulties they face in staying informed, but only when I ask the final question, regarding what is wrong with democracy today.

To be good citizens, informants repeatedly bring up the need to know more. Citizens ask for more information on how governance works. Informants talk about wanting to know how things are done, how negotiations occur, how decisions are made. This is a question of both educating the public about how the government works and maintaining open channels of communication between the public and elected officials. Citizens want to hear more about the governing processes and rationale behind decision making, in ways that evolve beyond the scripted vernacular of press officers and formal announcements. This trend is deeper than, and not addressed through, monitorial practices alone. Informants are deeply skeptical about the information they receive, which comes from many sources and frequently includes empty promises and rhetorical maneuvers.

The monitorial modality seems to delineate the contours of civic participation. It appears to be compatible, somewhat, with our daily routines. But is it a joyful mode of engagement? Does it lead to *areté*? It certainly fits the model of contemporary existence. It is sensitive to the scale of mass representative democracies. Still, informational policing for the purpose of potentially interfering in the event of wrongdoing is not necessarily something one gets excited about. And my informants get energized when they talk about the work they pour into their own micro-communities. They become inspired by stories of contribution to these communities. In the United States, community involvement is a persistent theme among black people, who frequently become more energized when talking about it. I am reminded of the words of Catherine Knight Steele and André Brock, both social scientists who delve into the practices of African American cybercultures. Knight Steele and Jessica Lu write about the idea of black joy: the affinity that black people have historically shown for mastering discourse to resist subjugation and oppression by dominant groups and their ability to do so increasingly online, in ways that celebrate black culture.[21] These narratives masterfully combine conflict, irreverence, seriousness, humor, sarcasm, and a variety of other conversational strategies that all result in forming a deep connective bond. Black joy is an illustration of the in-between bond that Arendt referred to. The monitorial modality is useful. Is it joyful?

On one hand, the monitorial modality is a reasonable approach to the contemporary demands of democratic governance and works in a variety of environments. On the other hand, over time, this modality of surveillance may gradually nullify paths of civic engagement. Think of these paths as marked by desire lines. The more often they are trod, the more visible they become. The more potent they are, the more memorable, the more accessible. The less often they are traveled, the dustier they become and thus the less visible they are when we, the monitorial citizens, need to intervene.

Other questions come to mind too. The monitorial model works as long as the information accessed is accurate, valid, reliable, deep, diverse, and trustworthy. Once the informational base becomes polluted, the monitorial capabilities of the citizen are compromised. And indeed they have been, as our increasing skepticism about the media, politics, and our representatives shows.

So what do we do when paths to civic engagement are compromised and when conduits to civic intervention become congested or obstructed? In search of good citizenship, some people engage in a monitorial or ambient mode, perusing the political infoscape on news feeds and ready to be mobilized if needed.[22] Many find civic joy in the micro practices pursued within their communities. The craftsman, or *homo faber*, presents a long-lost model of citizenry focused on the pleasure gained from doing things and doing things well.[23]

Sennett, in his later work, presented this as a way of offering a civic path to citizenship within a democracy dominated by capitalist models of production. As the public man fell, the craftsman, or doer, emerged. There is a masculine aesthetic to the conceptualization of these models that is not intentional but is present. I find the concept of black joy more meaningful in describing the sentiments derived from the pleasures of doing. And these sentiments resonate around the world. Valeria, in St. Petersburg, continues the story she told me earlier about a doctor she had encountered who said to her, "I will never be a famous person in the history book, but I want to be an important person to my community." She then followed him outside, and everybody would turn and say hello to him. She realized that "famous in a history book he might not be, but he was already as important, if not more, to his community as other people of fame." The ordinary, everyday virtues of tolerance, forgiveness, trust, and resilience drive people within the moral order of democracy to do good.[24] Good citizenship is connected to notions of altruism and shared visions of democracy and cooperation.[25]

These are just some of the micro civic practices that frequently fly under the radar, for they do not fit into our conventional categorizations of civic duty. They do not require voting and are often enacted because the practice of voting has yielded disappointing results. They sometimes involve play, but my informants rarely speak about these practices. I wonder if it is because they have been socialized into regarding them as non-civic. Still, I want to make space to talk about the political relevance of memes and GIFs that we retweet, like, or otherwise share and the affective bonds these enable. It is important to emphasize the importance of play, fun, and satire in a democracy, as these serve the purpose of emotional release and of breaking the ice and talking about difficult issues. The people I have studied all my life are playful. They use the internet and other media to poke fun at themselves and others and to reinvent civic practices that they find boring.[26] Sometimes these behaviors are for fun. Other times they are impromptu efforts aimed at using sarcasm, humor, or play as a way to claim a place in the conversation. Play is performative, as it utilizes a number of favorite routines, online and offline.[27] And it can become a way of accessing power, even if transitionally so.

Citizenship is performed, and these performances of citizenship render the citizen. Thinking leads to speech acts, which lead to enactments and assembled performances of citizenship. These performances are further rethought, reimagined, modified, remediated, and reenacted.[28] Whether citizens are reified as agents of civility rests on both dialogic and dialectic practices that develop.

It should not surprise us that citizens are restless in the contemporary civic environment and seek civic release elsewhere. Representative democracy enforces a homogeneity of public opinion through voting that emphasizes majority rule, which precludes any possibility of true pluralism. The political scientist Chantal Mouffe has famously labeled this the "democratic paradox," the inevitability that respect for the will of the majority will lead to the stifling of true plurality.[29] Most political scientists subscribe to the more tempered viewpoint that, while civic engagement in a representative democracy is not an impossibility, it is, nonetheless, a compromise.[30] Indeed, the majority of responses from my conversation companions are a result of a long process of democratic compromises that has left many of them skeptical about the future of democracy.

Still, Mouffe finds that the democratic paradox does not pose insurmountable challenges. She explains that while a true plurality of opinion cannot exist in a system that organizes voices into majority percentages, the real danger lies in framing minority opinions as antagonistic to majority ones. This creates unfortunate binaries and divisions that qualify the majority as winning and further marginalizes minority viewpoints. Citizens should not antagonize each other for winning the majority argument, and neither should politicians. Antagonism runs counter to the democratic premise of plurality, for it imposes a hierarchy of opinion contrary to deliberation. If deliberation is to bring us closer to informed consensus, then the antagonistic debate is useless. Mouffe has proposed "agonistic pluralism" as a "vibrant clash of democratic political positions," guided by undecidability and more receptive to the plurality of voices that develop within contemporary pluralist societies than the deliberative model. Specifically, the " 'agonistic' approach acknowledges the real nature of its frontiers and the forms of exclusion that they entail, instead of trying to disguise them under the veil of rationality or morality."[31] This more nuanced understanding of public opinion places the person firmly in the political and locates the individual at the heart of deliberative politics. Whereas debates, for example, imply a winner and a loser and thus are antagonistic by nature, deliberation is meant to lead to a form of agreement in which there are no winners or losers, nor is there compromise. There is agreement, which can be reached only if all parties approach civic affairs from an undecided position. It is a provocative position for several reasons. First, the position of undecidability has conventionally been associated with a lack of an opinion or interest, but Mouffe instead advocates for undecidability that rests on openness. Second, although some issues are open to undecidability, there are others, having to do with basic civil rights that all humans must enjoy, that are not. Mouffe's emphasis on agonistic pluralism presumes that as a society, we have identified a set of core values that are representative of inalienable rights.

Still, this is not exactly what Mouffe is after. She advocates that we embrace and understand conflict as a natural state of being and as a necessary condition for consensus. Without conflict, we cannot reach an agreement. This may not negate democratic impact, as long as it prioritizes agonistic over antagonistic politics. Trolling, for example, is an antagonistic practice. It is aimed at obliterating the opponent's viewpoint by completely delegitimizing it through a variety of intimidating practices. It is aimed at marginalizing particular viewpoints to the point of invisibility.

Agonism, on the other hand, is aimed not at marginalizing but rather at decentralizing. Adversarial acts of subversion, for instance, reflect an agonistic mentality. In thinking about both playful and adversarial civic practices, I am reminded of the response that Silvia, from Romania, gave me when I asked her what democracy is: "Democracy is having the right to refuse to respond to your question! That is what democracy is!" she responded while looking at me slyly.

Mouffe talks about something she terms a "conflictual consensus."[32] She uses this term to describe a real confrontation based on a shared set of rules and despite disparate individual positions, much like Elizabeth Anderson's reimagining of equality. Mouffe defines agonism as a "we/they relation," where the conflicting parties, although acknowledging that they are adversaries, operate on a common symbolic ground and see themselves as belonging to the same association. In this context, "the task of democracy is to transform antagonism into agonism."[33] While agonists do not function outside the spectrum of the public sphere, they are less concerned with the public accord and more with self-expression and voicing disagreement. The Occupy movement, for example, criticized frequently for its lack of a core set of objectives, was a de facto agonistic movement. Its purpose was not to obliterate contrary viewpoints but rather to provide an opportunity for decentralization from the main economic ethos, to offer people who wanted something different the opportunity to stand up and be counted. MAGA, by contrast, while offering the same opportunity for folks to stand up and be counted, frequently takes positions that marginalize counterviews on immigration, trade, taxation, and social welfare and thus becomes antagonistic. The direct representation and subversive capabilities of online media enable agonistic expressions of dissent that do not necessarily empower citizens, but they do enhance democracy by decentralizing its core and opening it up to disagreement.

Referenda, for example, a popular mode lately of calling up public opinion on demand, are antagonistic. They offer binary options and polarize opinions as they pit them against each other. Similarly, algorithms, our everyday automated news curators, are antagonistic too, because they organize our feeds in a manner that forces issues, people, and voices to compete for our attention. Agonistically organized algorithms would emphasize civic literacy and transparency and plurality.[34] Referenda could be replaced with opportunities that invite joyful, playful, and more meaningful interaction between citizens.

In my conversations, I sense that citizens are wanting greater diversity in representation and programs that enhance and support plurality. There is a lingering mood of dissatisfaction with the civic tools and paths at hand. Citizens identify the disparity between what the popular vote indicates and how each region, state, or municipality is represented. The general sentiment is that representational equality would help citizens connect with elected officials and find ways to be more engaged and less skeptical.

The problem, I find, is not one of apathy and disillusionment. It is one of citizens striving to be agonistic in a world that invites them to be antagonistic. Let me put this in less theoretical terms: I find myself talking to people who want to volunteer their contributions to societies that operate by putting a price on everything. I listen to my interviews repeatedly and hear people who are eager to be involved yet are presented primarily with commercially driven ways of doing so. I hear the voices of citizens who offer inspirational stories yet are asked to reduce their nuanced opinions to yes-or-no responses. I talk with people who have lively personalities and imaginations yet are called to participate through civic paths that are formulaic, dry, and boring. Citizens want to be seen and heard. Contemporary democracies, unfortunately, render them invisible.

FOUR

Toward the New

Revolutions are nothing if not about new beginnings.[1] This chapter connects the responses people provide when I ask them what they would like to see change about democracy. I ask what they hope might be better about democracy and listen to nuanced stories about democracy's failures. Some responses are focused entirely on what has gone wrong. Others consider what might be different. None find democracy ideal. If chapter 2 was about voice and equality and chapter 3 about noble intentions rendered invisible in practice, then the consensus that emerges though conversations summarized in this chapter is this: little is right, and a lot must change.

Still, change is gradual, and revolutions are long.[2] And they have to be long, in order to attain meaning. Changing institutions involves first renegotiating their symbolic place in democracies. Many of the tiny acts of political participation described in the previous chapter form around the need to redefine how democratic institutions work. When people speak of contributing more to their own micro-communities through their everyday routines, they are actively engaging in a critique of how societal organizations work.

Likewise, when folks engage in online debates, share memes, reproduce slogans, and participate in movements, they engage in
efforts that have to do with renegotiating the meaning and impact
of democratic institutions. A movement like #BlackLivesMatter,
for instance, is not about making a statement that at first glance
seems obvious. The Black Lives Matter refrain is a symbolic re-
minder that despite assumed advances in civil rights, social injustice
persists. Likewise, the Occupy movement allowed people to stand
up and be counted, in articulating the general message that core aspects of societal organizations in democracies need to be rethought.
To change institutions, we must reimagine them first.[3] Citizens
communicate this through their everyday routines, although they
are rarely listened to.

Transition is a key element of change, and both often make people uneasy. All of the countries I traveled through as I met and conversed with people seemed to be undergoing some form of transition.
The United Kingdom went through two prime ministers and a po-
larizing nationwide debate on its future inside or outside the European Union. Greece had already pondered such a future and decided
to stay in the European Union, at great cost, with a struggling economy, and with elections always looming. In Brazil and Mexico, I interviewed people before and after elections that were both promising
and disappointing. In the United States, it seemed that we were realizing that we have always been polarized, even if we were unaware
of the extent. Germany went through an uneasy transition that
threatened the delicate balance its leadership has always observed
between extreme right-wing and extreme left-wing factions. In
Canada, the land the rest of the world often fantasizes about when
all else falls apart, people have their own list of disappointments and
unmet expectations.

The form of transition is a key aspect of effecting social change.[4]
The anthropologist Victor Turner, in studying social drama, conflict, and change, found that all societies go through the same pat-

tern of liminality when transitioning from one state of social order to the next. He thought of this process as a rite-of-passage progression, inclusive of stages of transition and in-between positions that individuals occupy. Turner understood liminality as a time of social and structural ambiguity, or as "the Nay to all positive structural assertions, but as in some sense the source of them all, and, more than that, as a realm of pure possibility whence novel configurations of ideas and relations may arise."[5] A group of liminal actors is characterized by a lack of social markers, and that renders all actors equal. This abandonment of hierarchy also permits activity that will result in the birthing of a new structure, and therein lie both potential empowerment and disempowerment. Turner understands "liminality as a phase in social life in which this confrontation between 'activity which has no structure' and its 'structured results' produces in men their highest pitch of self-consciousness."[6] Evanescent as this moment of heterarchy is, it is crucial to setting in motion the process of transitioning from one state to the next. It is often suggested that newer technologies afford such states of liminality, of broadly distributed and interconnected heterarchy that propagates movements.

The possibility of change rests on liminality, balances of power between different stakeholders, and windows of opportunity that may open.[7] Technology is not a solution; it offers a path to change but does not guarantee it. This is why none of my questions refer to it. I would prefer that my informants bring it up on their own, and some have so far.

What do people think about when they think about change? Power. Conversations revolve around access to information, misinformation, corruption, adjustments to the electoral system, money and politics, representation, and practices of listening. These responses tend to pick up where responses to the questions on democracy and citizenship drop off. Therefore, citizens return to conditions identified earlier, associated with representative inequality, information equality, transparency, and civic literacy. They connect these with further conditions that need to be put in place for literacy, transparency, and representation to work. Ultimately, these are all roundabout ways of talking about greater access to power or a redistribution of power.

Preliminary findings indicate that in general, citizens are disappointed by the knowledge elected officials possess on public affairs and issues of global import. They are uncertain as to whether it is honest ignorance or influence by lobbying special interests that lead politicians to vote against scientifically ascertained facts—issues that come up most frequently include vaccination, global warming, and a lack of understanding when it comes to the way new media technologies work. Informants often bring up the lack of *civic literacy for elected officials*. Some suggest that both pre- and post-election, officials should enter programs to educate them on the finer details of current and long-term important issues. Before running for office, candidates should have some type of civic training or certificate. Several countries in the European Union do subsidize such programs, focusing on diplomacy studies. In the United States, by contrast, there are very few programs focusing on international affairs, and they are offered by private or public universities to tuition-paying students. Still, a handful of foreign-service or international-affairs programs are state subsidized in Australia, Mexico, Japan, Peru, Ghana, and South Korea. Such programs could be expanded, feature more focused training, and become more prevalent and affordable to all, so as to avoid reproducing class division. My conversational companions reiterate that all too often they are asked to choose among candidates they do not deem capable, educated, or knowledgeable. The point many are making is that we cannot have officials who are not as well educated or informed as the citizens voting for them to govern us. We must elect our finest.

Moreover, in identifying what might change, informants tend to show a preference for the logistics of city-states, smaller states, and smaller democracies. They point toward a reorganization and

rescaling of governance that would enable and empower more direct forms of democracy. *Reorganizing and rethinking democracies* are
frequently brought up in this context. I have heard a variety of options, including national forms of governance that could center
more on management and less on decision making. In so doing,
elected officials at the national and global levels may become experts
in conflict management, reconciliation, and negotiation. Local representatives might spend more time in regional politics. Journalism
and other channels would emerge to connect local, regional, and
national levels of governance.

Compellingly, informants talk about preserving democracy. They
bring up caring and looking after democracy, as if it were something
to be cherished, valued, and protected. There is a growing sense
that those who are in power have a different understanding of what
democracy is. Certainly, there is a disconnect between the people
and those who govern, and democracy is about eliminating this disconnect, not reinforcing it.

A Tale of Populism

When we report the results of democratic processes, the convention
has it that we frequently use the phrase "by popular vote." By popular vote, policies are approved, officials are elected, and decisions are
made. Still, what is popular, and is the popular also democratic? The
popular vote marks the options that have been endorsed by the most
people and thus a path forward that reflects a majority, although not
a plurality, of voices. Not everyone's viewpoint is represented by the
popular vote or by what is popular generally. By contrast, history has
taught us that the popular vote frequently endorses practices that go
against human decency. Silent majorities have historically been
incapable of reversing paths that lead to crimes against humanity.

The popular route is both exciting and dangerous: exciting precisely because it does embrace the desires of the many, dangerous because the will of the majority can easily be exploited and is sometimes

determined not by what we want but by what is available. This last point becomes a resounding refrain as I converse with people around the world. "People confuse politics, culture, and democracy; they are not the same, and pop culture gets in the way," says Mamie, an African American woman and former office administrator who had once run for mayor in her home city of Chicago. She is trying to tell me that what is popular is not always necessarily what is best for people.

Yet what is popular is often used to lure the attention, stir the emotions, and capture the votes of citizens, and my companions in this global conversation are aware of both this tendency and the obstacles to fighting it. Uzma, a refugee from Pakistan, talks with me at length about how leaders use the will of the people as an excuse to act in their own interest: "People go for fame, and the majority follows." Umair, one of Uzma's friends, also from Pakistan, adds that "populists prevail, leaders make promises, and people are swayed," when in fact "people should think of the progress of the state, not their own, when voting." Khrilid from Morocco talks with me about the many ways in which politicians pay for votes, concluding, "People want more choice; often people have to choose the least worst." Nikos from Greece rounds up this virtually connected conversation circle with this comment: "We must balance emotion and logic to be good citizens . . . so as to avoid populism." Referenda often convey the promise of direct democracy and immediate choice but also are exploited by populist rhetoric. Citizens recognize this tendency, and while they are open to referenda, they also appreciate ones that offer more numerous, nuanced options beyond yes/no binaries, as both Carine from Germany and Thomas from the United Kingdom agree.

So what is *populism*, and how exactly does it connect to the popular? Ernesto Laclau, a political theorist well known for his work on the topic, understood populism as a dialectic, a political logic that could be co-opted by a variety of right-wing, centrist, or left-wing ideologies. He and his long-term partner, Chantal Mouffe, often wrote about the importance of liberty and equality. They found that it was important not only to value these two concepts but also to keep democracy vibrant and alive by fighting over them and redefining what they mean constantly. This was the only way to allow democracy to evolve with us, and it leads to Mouffe's idea of agonistic pluralism, which I have already connected to contemporary citizens.

It is telling that Laclau titled his most influential work on populism *On Populist Reason*. Some people presume that populism lacks reason, but Laclau argued that it has a logic, that it is a progression of its own. Populists rely on discourse and utilize refrains to attract attention and distract from the complexity of issues. Laclau explained that populists often use *empty signifiers* to allow the masses to connect around abstract ideas. The term is rooted in the work of the famous philosopher Antonio Gramsci, who was imprisoned for his beliefs by the Mussolini fascist regime in Italy in the mid-1920s.[8] Gramsci is better known for explaining how cultural processes often reinforce and reproduce popular points of view, reinforcing hegemony, a form of ideological superiority that permits elites to claim and retain power over others, in both democratic and non-democratic regimes. The semiotician Claude Lévi-Strauss uses the term "open" or "floating signifier" to describe terms that lack any real meaning and thus are open to multiple interpretations.[9]

Laclau, influenced by both Gramsci and Lévi-Strauss, explained how empty signifiers can be used to reproduce and reinforce popular ideas by the united publics behind these affective refrains. An empty signifier works to promote populism because it lacks any true ideological potency. It has a very abstract meaning, so it allows people to align behind an abstract idea, to interpret it in a way that does not contradict their own beliefs, and to offer their support for it. Brexit is a contemporary signifier. It is an abstraction that allows people to unite, despite their own complex feelings and reasons for wanting to leave the European Union. The term itself offers no solutions, nor does it invite complex discussion. It permits people to affectively tune in, stand up, and be counted as supportive of a general idea. MAGA,

Make America Great Again, is yet another empty signifier. It is an abstract idea that is, by definition, difficult to disagree with—no U.S. citizen would want to make America bad, for instance. It is thus an empty slogan, with no meaning. People line up behind it and fill it with their own meanings and interpretations, as they gather and offer their support to an idea that is too general to point to a specific policy yet broad enough not to leave anyone excluded (by definition).

As populist rhetoric emerges, it makes frequent use of empty signifiers as slogans. It is difficult for a populist strategy to work without an affective refrain of its own. These refrains are usually introduced by a leading figure, someone who, per Laclau, is frequently anointed a populist messiah: an individual who rhetorically and emotionally connects with a crowd and emerges as someone who can magically put an end to all problems. Every era, country, and context have their own populist messiahs. They are elevated to prominence through mechanisms that combine interpersonal conversational conventions with traditional practices of broadcasting opinion. In so doing, populists seek to both circumvent and exploit traditional channels of communication that are prevalent in a democracy. Therefore, it is not uncommon to see populist leaders engage with the mainstream to provoke attention and evoke messianic rhetoric of promise.[10] They do so by utilizing an empty signifier of symbolic significance and employing an independent channel to further disrupt democratic practices and engage in direct communication with constituents.[11] In so doing, populists explain that they are pushing aside intermediaries who are polluting the purity of their message and create binaries, divisions that thrive on an *us versus them* mentality.

How does one resist ever-present populist tendencies? I am not sure that any measures can be taken to completely eradicate appeals to the popular. We will always fantasize about easy solutions and be dazzled by enticing rhetoric. Populists emerge out of all sorts of ideological corners, and no measure of education can render any of us completely immune to them. We will always have populism. It is a permanent flaw of democracy. It will never go away. Majority rule has populism as its obligatory companion, in societies democratic and non-democratic, capitalist or other. Populism thrives on insecurity. We often go through overwhelming waves of populism following periods of long financial instability. It is during those times that invite desperation that people are most likely to fall prey to solutions presented as easy, no matter how abstract.

Still, once we accept populism as a permanent state or, better yet, as a permanent virus of democracy, then we learn how to treat it; we develop antibodies for it. And we develop defense mechanisms. How does one make democracy better? The first theme that emerges, across all respondents, is to "lose populism," in the words of Louis from Mexico. It seems that people realize that populism is connected to ego and insecurity, as several of my informants talk about setting aside personal interest and individual insecurities and choosing leaders who make honest promises. Regina, from Brazil, tells me that democracy can only get better through the election of honest people who are really committed to the needs of the population.

One of my interviewees, Hussein, fled from Afghanistan and the Taliban, and he presciently tells me that democracy needs stability, financial but really all types of stability, to thrive. Insecurity is at the root of many problems, including political ones. Confidence, on the other hand, and inclusivity are openly embraced by many of my informants as the way out of a populist rut. You have to "let democracies breathe, open the door for undemocratic types to come in. You can't force democracy. It invites all types of leaders. It is more fragile than we think," says Drew from New York. Indeed, it is fragile, despite its resilience, as are many things in life.

The Toll of Corruption

The first theme that emerges as I talk with people about the problems of contemporary democracy concerns a problem both old and new: the difficulty of endorsing the popular vote without amplifying populist tendencies. The second theme is equally familiar and concerns the challenges that rise up as we try to reconcile the popular vote with what is financially viable. People often speak of corruption as if it is something new or specific to their own sociocultural context. That is not the case, as there is no political-economic structure that is not susceptible to corruption. Corruption is the result of human behaviors amounting to dishonesty. Systemic factors may render it easy; but they are not responsible for it, and they cannot extinguish it entirely. Like many of the problems of democracy, corruption is a long-term companion.

In talking about corruption, people acknowledge its different faces and causes readily. During my conversations, I hear about dishonesty being the primary problem in democracy and politics today. Michael, an energetic retiree from the United States and possibly the oldest of my conversational companions, roots for honesty and transparency as he tells me that "politicians should be honest with what they think, . . . be who you are, and not say things just because you want to be elected. Don't choose your principles based on lobbies." Kristi from Greece and Ecuador begins her conversation with me calmly and cynically, by bluntly telling me that democracy does not really exist anywhere because of corruption and abuse of power. This long history of abusing power has led to a disillusionment with the practice of voting, she continues. People see no meaning to the practice of voting and, therefore, often see no reason to vote. Similarly, Umair and Uzma seem to think it more likely that governments will be crooked than honest and thus spend much of their time with me talking about the obligation of citizens to be vigilant and aware and to call politicians to task. Policing corrupt politicians is no one's favorite pastime, and the need to be on the lookout for it leaves people longing for transparency, immediacy, and more honest communication, says Karina, from Uzbekistan. When there is corruption, people have no choice but disillusionment, she adds. Khrilid directly tells me that in his native country of Morocco, politicians pay for votes. Hiba and Lucian from Syria talk about the many different ways of paying for votes and exerting pressure on citizens and call for greater freedom in voting.

The talk of corruption is endless and monopolizes the conversation once it begins. Gone are the long pauses and the textbook definitions of citizenship. Talk of corruption produces torrents of indignant responses. "Voting is too complicated," chimes in Annett from Germany. Lobbyists and big companies have disproportionate power to citizens' voting, elaborates Carina, a German banker in her early sixties. The country is run by "a lot of people with money who have their hands dipped into their pockets," says Mark, from the United States. "It is sadly what drives our society. . . . It is what people want. People want money," he finally concludes, with a sense of resignation. "If you have money, you will have a strong voice, in this ongoing weird cycle of 'I need your money, but what do you need for this money?' " This idea drives our democracy, he further adds. "Take corporate money out of it," chimes in Nathan, from Canada. "How do you make democracy better?" I ask Renice, from the United States, a feisty buildings and grounds manager who looks at me through her piercing, knowing eyes that make me feel like the most naive person on the planet. You get "people to stop being crooked," she snaps. And then she quickly adds, "Good luck with that."

Talk quickly turns to the electoral process and how its mechanisms often invite or amplify corruption. Cliff, from the United States, talks about the lack of political options, with interests often grouped in two broad opposing categories, leaving citizens feeling underrepresented: "We have been grouped into one of two categories when there is a lot of gray area in between." Matthew, a retired school psychologist from Pennsylvania, gets passionate as he talks about broadening the options voters are presented with by getting "moncy out of the process of selecting our representatives." His criticism is accompanied by a solution, as he suggests shortening the period of campaigning and allocating money for public funding of elections. Nathan points to the same problem, explaining that the election season is shorter in his home country of Canada, and this certainly lessens voter fatigue.

I am reminded of the work of many scholars, most notably Thomas Patterson, a political scientist based at Harvard who spent most of his career tracking how the elongated campaigning process in the United States disadvantages democratic processes and alienates the public. In his famous book *Out of Order*, he described how a campaigning process that begins two years prior to the event of the presidential elections in the United States requires that candidates generate inordinately large campaign budgets, typically by aligning themselves with special interests and lobbying groups. Politicians then embark on a lengthy campaign process that leaves them, the media, and citizens exhausted. The media resort to covering elections as competitions, frequently using horse-race mentality and vocabulary to sustain ratings over the long campaign. In-depth coverage of issues decreases as reporters are disillusioned by a process that requires them to follow candidates who repeat the same promises, stump speeches, and handshake politics on the campaign trail. Citizens also get tired of listening to the same narratives over and over again, and the lack of substantive coverage further renders them cynical toward the media and politicians.[12] Patterson's recommendation was very similar to Matthew's and involved shortening the campaign period and introducing greater transparency in the allocation of campaign funds.

Still, the narrative of a long campaign, at least in the United States, persists, and it thrives on generating ratings by presenting the positions of the candidate as irreconcilable and distinct. The effect is to amplify "polarization and antagonism, an environment where everybody hates everybody," as Michael, from the United States, points out. These comments resonate with informants across the globe, whose experiences reflect different electoral processes and varying media systems but the same concern about polarization, toxicity, and antagonism—all motivated by the desire to game the economic system. Louis, the cab driver from Mexico City, gets agitated as he talks about corruption, which is culturally embedded. It is not a problem that can be regulated away. Olga, a pharmacist from Greece, talks about the importance of honesty in politics. Xheni, a refugee from Albania, blurts out "corruption" before I am even finished articulating the question. Hamid from Ghana talks about wanting to work, wanting to give one's best, but having corruption always get in the way. Ekaterina from Russia tells me that democracy is great but is doomed to be an impossible utopia, rendered inaccessible because of corruption.

Talk of corruption in the electoral process quickly gets more specific as respondents discuss special interests influencing campaigns, privileging candidates, and using money to make certain voices louder than others. As my interviews progress across the United States, I listen to more and more complaints about gerrymandering and how it has exacerbated the problem of polarization in politics. Yet when I return home from the interviews and turn to the television or go online to get the news, I get the same language from politicians, and I hear the same vague responses to questions on the firm place capital holds in the democratic process. People speak with me about the lack of loyalty and trust and about companies becoming involved in politics in ways that hurt the rights of the elderly, students, patients, and veterans. The system needs to have the best interest of all in mind, and all my conversational companions, no matter their ideological affiliation, find that the financial hegemony of capitalism has failed at this. This sentiment is echoed by the feeling that increasingly, in Michael's words, "corporations have unlimited financial influence in elections, and that really goes against one person one vote because now special interests have a louder voice."

Beyond the United States, the calls for reform are also echoed by a tepid acknowledgment that these programs might require greater taxation. No one is eager to pay more taxes, however, and the emphasis seems to be placed on taxation being scaled so that those who are more privileged, including corporations, are taxed at higher rates to contribute a greater part of their wealth to improving social conditions for all, rather than furthering their own interests. This is the resounding chorus that follows me as I travel and speak with people of different backgrounds. Capitalism is at odds with democracy, and yet both capitalism and democracy are all we have. We do not have alternatives, and it seems that the stronger the position of capitalism becomes, the weaker the hold of democracy on governance comes to be. We need capitalism to be softer for democracy to be stronger.

How does capitalism get soft while remaining profitable? This is not an insurmountable problem, but it does require creative thinking. I am not the only scholar to point out the incompatibility of democracy and capitalism or to recognize the lunacy of expecting the two to be compatible partners. Most of our problems arise from the fact that our two prevailing systems for economic and political organization are deeply at odds with each other. This does not mean that they cannot be redesigned to work better together.

The historical developments of the past century have made it obvious that capitalism is here to stay but has given rise to movements expressing deep dissatisfaction with capitalism. The Occupy and Indignados movements present the most recent examples. Discontent with capitalism dates back to early worker movements at the dawn of the industrialization era and, even before that, as smaller factions of workers organized against disproportionate distributions of wealth that resulted as markets were manipulated by a variety of economic and political agents. I do not find that markets can magically produce a fair distribution of wealth through the notorious invisible hand of competition. Competition is beneficial for societies, and it thrives in markets. Markets, however, like all platforms, contain bias, and bias inadvertently or intentionally skews balance, advantages some actors, and is prone to exploitation. Markets, to paraphrase what Melvin Kranzberg famously said about technology, are a form of technology, and as such, they are neither good nor bad, nor are they neutral.[13]

Social scientists and increasingly economists are concerned with reforming capitalist mechanisms to make them more compatible with democracy and to bring them up to date. It is not just democracy that needs a do-over. We are stuck with a dominant model of capitalism that took on its core shape sometime in the 1700s. It worked from an economy that traded products. We spent most of the twentieth century trading services, and we are going to spend our future trading, primarily, information. If we do not reorganize the foundational market structure, we are going to keep on trading information based on standards that were put into effect centuries ago, and in so doing, we will keep producing, reinforcing, and eventually bursting financial bubbles, cycles of intense development that lead to exacerbated and overestimated gain only to be followed by periods of disproportionate loss as profit margins adjust to normal. Kate from Canada talks about how she frequently struggles with the ageism of the democratic system and its inability to account for the wants, needs, and habits of young people. Anna talks about how "in Canada, democracy fails with regard to marginalized populations, [with] not counting indigenous populations into politics. . . . And the other problem is that it is based on a majority, so that limits things." Nathan, also from Canada, picks up on this point and talks about working locally and with smaller communities, in a manner that reminds me of what Valeria had mentioned in St. Petersburg: "There is so much emphasis on federal that we lose focus of the smaller things."

To this end, the work of Eric Posner and Glen Weyl on "radical markets" becomes quite relevant and presents some contemporary options.[14] The term "radical" here is not used to introduce an utter reversal of both economic and political systems in place. The authors acknowledge the importance and relevance of markets and the central place capitalism occupies as a dominant mode of financial organization. Their efforts are not organized around usurping capitalism but rather focused on adjusting, fixing, correcting, and updating it. Posner and Weyl, whose efforts began with a book and quickly spawned a multitude of partnerships of local and national governments, are interested in making politics more compatible with the economy and adjusting capitalism so that it is better equipped to support democracy. They propose a variety of soft adjustments, several focused on more nuanced equations of taxation than the more rigid formulas of taxation corresponding to income levels that we have grown accustomed to. And they further propose ways of voting and participating in politics that permit people to have a stronger voice on issues they have a greater stake in, by virtue of their proximity, heritage, and sociocultural status.

It is a complex model that relies on community organization on the micro level that restores the in-between bonds that Hannah Arendt famously spoke of. The meso- and macro levels use loose yet transparent bonds to facilitate collaboration between micro-communities. It is a way to allow democracy, a system custom made for small societies, to scale up in a way that does not sacrifice its substance. Further, it is a program that allows capitalism, a system that thrives on placing the individual above the collective, to reconcile an individual want with the needs of the collective. It permits an economic organization to yield gain as it attains economies of scale but also to scale up in a manner that is humane, resulting in what I refer to as soft capitalism, strong democracy. This model, along with my own ideas, are developed further in the next chapter. Before I get there, I would like to talk about the last major theme that emerges as I speak with people about what ails democracy and what might make it better.

An Education

At the conclusion of my interviews, people often ask me what I have been finding so far. They are interested in how people from other countries define democracy or citizenship. They are even more eager to hear whether people across the world share the same concerns. In the process of researching this book, I also visited a variety of community organizations, private-sector firms, and educational institutions. I was eager to share my findings and ideas and hear the recommendations and advice of others. As I told people I was working on this book, the question I was asked most often was, "What do people say about social media? Or the news media?"

"Nothing," I typically responded and laughed as they gave me a look of surprise in return. But it is true. My conversational companions rarely bring up news media or social media as core problems of democracy. When news and social media emerge in conversation, they appear toward the end, and they are always connected to the greater issue of an educated public, consisting of informed citizens and informed politicians. When I ask people, "What is wrong with democracy?" people talk about populism and corruption at great length. I am a scholar of technology. I have spent my entire career studying how technology affects political processes and society. I am always ready to talk about the media, yet for the first time in my career, I find myself speaking with people who want to talk about anything but.

People first talk about the need for education. Naturally what comes to mind is equal access to information of a diverse and accurate nature. For all of my informants, information is central to performing their civic duties. So naturally, when they are bombarded with misinformation, they are confused, disillusioned, and indignant. Still, rarely do they solely blame the media. They point their finger at politicians and special interests first. Stanley, a middle-aged facilities director from the United States, begins by telling me that "democracy has to be credible. We need to get accurate information. We can't have a voice, stake in the game, and be heard without credible information." This information has to "be pure, unfiltered, and with integrity, not plowed with commercialism and all else," he continues, as I hear the indignation growing in his typically calm demeanor during his final statement: "Commercialism gets in the way of communication." Commercialism rules in the United States, and it often gets in the way of applying checks and balances, of enhancing communication, of providing transparently generated information.

Commercialism invites misinformation, and this becomes a familiar theme in my conversations in the United States. There is "so much information out there and, equally, misinformation there [that] I just can't believe everything that I am reading," says Stanley, before confessing, "I'm getting stuck—there is 10 percent accurate info out there, and the rest is garbage." Estella from Canada emphasizes accessibility and civic engagement being key to how media enhance democracies: "Reporting is reactive; it should be proactive!" she asserts.

The lack of accurate information forces people into a position of helplessness that they are reluctant to maintain and exasperated that they have to resort to. "We don't always understand how people are elected into office, . . . what our vote means," muses Nancy from Canada before she recommends that "we follow the money, so as to understand what is going on. . . . That is what the media are supposed to do." Elizabeth, a registered nurse from the United States, loosens up during the interview to confide, "As I am getting older, I become more opinionated, and I don't like that." "I see unfairness, and I want to point it out," she continues, as she becomes more agitated and explains that she wants someone to come into office who is educated. Not everyone is fit for politics, she says. Have them all take a civics test, politicians and voters, and "make them all anonymous, then vote for whoever's thoughts you like."

It is around this focus on education for a politician that all the voices around the world begin to connect. I am surprised to find that people do not complain about the media or their own lack of education as much as they complain about having to choose between politicians who are not adequately educated themselves. And education means so much more than being able to discern between what is fact and what is fake news, as Monica from the United States tells me. It is about being able to read and listen to opposing views, and this would ultimately lead to democracy being more enlightened.

Chen, a technology worker based in Hangzhou, talks about the importance of an education for politicians and citizens alike. Viktor, from Russia, talks about lifelong learning and the importance of learning from our mistakes as we participate in the electoral process. Mamie, from Chicago, echoes this thought as she talks about people allowing themselves to mature and teach themselves to behave like civic adults. The more people talk, the clearer the emergent theme becomes: it is not people who lack the education to vote; it is the leaders who lack the education to govern.

"Elections should not be a popularity contest," Fiona from Albania exclaims, as she talks about often having to choose between the lesser of two evils. She suggests that leaders be tested on their ability to govern, on their knowledge, and on their empathy levels. Laura from Greece adds that leaders should be sensible and sensitive, for they are presently too far removed from the public. "There is such a big gap between the public and elected officials," she claims, to which Fiona, nearby, adds, "It's like a broken telephone game." Not everyone is fit for office, Kristi explains, and Karina, who has fled from Uzbekistan, emphasizes that the people who govern us must have experience, education, and knowledge. Olga from Greece says that things are too easy; we must raise the standards, and we must apply strict criteria for voting.

As the conversation continues, it becomes clear that an education is absent from the background of most politicians we have to choose from. It also becomes apparent that with education, citizens expect greater knowledge about public affairs but, beyond that, a greater sense of respect for democracy and the polity. Underneath this demand for education lies the need for respect and a call for politicians who can use their knowledge to set the right tone for difficult conversations between opposing viewpoints that must take place in democracies. There is a growing lack of respect and venom toward people who do not profess what you do, says Martha, a retired physician from the United Kingdom, who admits that somewhere along the line we got a little sidetracked and that this atmosphere of toxicity cannot go on forever.

Populism, corruption, and the need for civic literacy emerge as central trends that prevent citizens from feeling they are part of a healthy democracy. They are contemporary problems, but they are not new. They are long-standing conditions. People bring up different examples of populism and corruption and suggest varying avenues to education and civic agency. The tonality, language, and expression change as I travel, but the core themes persist. The song remains the same. As I listen to my informants, I think about the number of times they have shared these concerns with others throughout their lifetimes. I consider the number of people who have complained about corruption over the centuries. I lose track as I count the number of times populist rhetoric has swayed our minds and hearts. I realize that we have never been adequately educated to carry the burden of democracy and question that we ever will feel sufficiently literate. I am not sure there is a way out of cycles of toxicity that have been reproduced for years. How can we achieve the next stage of democracy?

FIVE

Before Democracy

If the recent past is any indication, this book will be published as populist tensions and tendencies reorganize how we think about democracy. It will be read in the context of elections that involve misinformation and disinformation campaigns carried out by humans, governments, and artificially intelligent agents. The moment will be characterized by polarization, ambivalence, and confusion. The title of this book, *After Democracy*, may imply that these developments will lead to an undoing of democracy. But that was never my intention, and it was not the starting point of this book. As I have tried to make clear, we have always struggled with democracy. I was inspired by moments when I saw democracy work well and events that drove deliberative processes forward. I did not write this book because I saw democracy collapsing and wanted to prevent its demise. On the contrary, I arrived at the idea for this book because I thought that after centuries with democracy, we might perhaps consider how it could transform into an advanced mode of governance. I was curious about what might follow democracy at its zenith, not its nadir moment.

And then I traveled, and I found myself first in countries like Mexico and Brazil where democracy was being stretched to its limits, by candidates who had exploited the faith of the people through populist agendas. Soon referenda and elections in the United Kingdom and the United States brought to light tensions that had been concealed beneath the rhythms of democratic conventions. The tone and tenor of politics in the United Kingdom and the United States evolved into a mix of stubbornness, authoritarianism, and mis- or disinformation. These developments strangely overlapped with the political travails I listened to while traveling in Russia and China, regimes that are both often characterized as authoritarian in the West. My native country of Greece was emerging out of a crisis brought on by economic insecurity but with vast democratic repercussions, ones that led people to elect extremist factions into parliament and have them partner with communist parties in a shocking alliance. It was populist rhetoric and economic insecurity that had brought Greece into that odd set of circumstances, back in 2009.

How oddly serendipitous that I would witness the same combination of populism and insecurity take its toll through the rest of the world and, specifically, the countries I was visiting for this project. There was Canada, recently regarded as a democratic haven but not considered quite that by its own citizens. And finally, there were the refugees, from everywhere but mostly from countries that had laid the foundation for civilization, philosophy, and democracy to grow. The irony there, of course, was that the refugees were the tragic outcome of a wave of revolutionary uprisings that shook the Middle Eastern and North African region in 2010 and onward. The West was quick to project its own democratic aspirations on these uprisings. These expectations quickly devolved into geopolitical conflicts that were more about the natural resources and strategic partnerships with those countries and less about democratic ideals.

This was a set of developments I was familiar with, for much of my work has traced how technology aids, obstructs, or transforms democracies, movements, and non-democratic regimes. And technology certainly had its own part to play in how revolutions were sold to an expectant Western public, how conflicts were framed in the news media, who was blamed for the financial crisis through cycles of mis- and disinformation, and most strikingly, how technology amplified the voices of the marginalized but also magnified the message of the populists.

So here I was, trying to predict what might follow democracy. I embarked on this research from a place of earnest curiosity about what others made of democracy. I expected cynicism because our research on democracy and technology reveals an increasingly cynical public. It became immediately apparent that solving the problem of democracy was irrevocably connected to finding a way to eliminate that cynicism and restore mechanisms of trust. As I suggested earlier in this book, skepticism is a natural, healthy development, to be expected from people who are educated and experienced and who think about democracy. Skepticism is not bad; it reveals knowledge and foresight. Cynicism, on the other hand, is skepticism with a serious dose of poignancy, and the latter is not something that disappears all that easily. A series of positive experiences are needed to counter the demeanor of publics that are not just skeptical but also cynical.

My conversational companions often hesitated when I asked them what democracy meant to them. They took some time to ponder the question of what being a citizen means in contemporary societies. Yet it took them no time to respond when I asked them what was wrong with democracy and what might make it better. I would argue that the ambivalence in defining citizenship and democracy was not connected to a lack of knowledge. It was reflective of cynicism, skepticism, and disillusionment.

The same ambivalence did not seem to hinder my companions from identifying the core of most problems plaguing the regimes I traveled through, democratic or non-democratic. Throughout my travels, my informants found that corruption, populism, and the lack of civic literacy hampered democracies from functioning properly. These three things also kept people from getting to their civic duties: corruption, populism, and lack of education. These may seem obvious, but it should bother us that the answers to a problem that we have long struggled to solve are so evident and yet so insurmountable.

How does one solve problems that have lasted for centuries? We must treat these problems like we treat a chronic disease. We must diagnose, treat, take proactive measures, and monitor, allowing time for our interventions to work. Connecting my companions' responses, I hope this book can offer the diagnosis.

Democracy at a Dead End

The following five themes emerged as my conversations evolved around the globe: silence and noise, familiarity and ambivalence, equality, voice, and skepticism. All five themes reflect the indecision with which citizens approach the question of democracy. Starting with the silence that almost always followed my posing of the initial question to the skepticism that eventually emerged as my participants came up with an answer, uncertainty permeated the tone of the conversation. This was the feeling that was shared among respondents and across geographic boundaries, a communal silence that oddly weaved their perspectives together.

I explained how striking this initial silence was when encountered across different cultural contexts dealing with varying levels of political turmoil—silence as pensiveness, pause for thought. *Silence* amid the *noise* of turmoil reflected the emotional dead end that was the starting point of this conversation. *Familiarity* and *ambivalence* surfaced as people attempted to define democracy. In doing so, they resorted to familiar definitions, typically with a measure of reluctance. They were aware they were providing token responses and conflicted that they could not access a vocabulary that would permit them to evolve beyond the expected.

Inevitably, all efforts to reach a definition of democracy arrived at and were simultaneously halted by the discussion of *equality*. Democracy does not guarantee that we are free; it ensures that we are equally free—or at least it provides avenues to equality that afford access for all without impeding progress for others. This is an impossible task, especially given changes in customs, technology, lifestyles, and economic conditions.

Pluralism, for example, enabled by new media, affords access to all but not on equal terms and often in ways that restrict people's preferences for connection and expression. Platforms like Twitter and Facebook both amplify our voice and rob us of the nuance of context. They collapse all of our spheres of interaction into one, frequently taking away the flexibility we have to be one type of person at work, a different type with our friends, and yet another version of that self in our intimate lives. Equality always means the same thing, but the path to equality differs as we cross social, cultural, and public or private spheres of interaction that are uniquely defined. Platforms that afford a democratic architecture for interaction must respect those boundaries and give equal autonomy to delineate them. Some paths to equality have been paved, yet more still need to be mapped out. We often define equality as access to certain things, and so, in order to understand what equality stands for in contemporary times, we must constantly reexamine it. As our habits change, our pathways for equality must flex, adjust, and expand, as should our laws, constitutions, and mandates—so that we can define and protect in a way that is reconcilable with our present and future. Guarantees to equality that worked twenty years ago may no longer be functional, and infrastructure that had been put into place must be revisited and updated constantly.

Once that is accomplished, equal access to *voice* means nothing if no one is prepared or interested in listening to us. While the emphasis is often placed on access, more attention must be directed to reciprocal or even multidimensional avenues for communication. Citizens are concerned that they are not heard, both because their voices are not loud enough and because the media and politicians are not listening. Moreover, they are summoned to express opinions through formats that do not afford much room for the richness of personal opinion. Referenda and polls narrow down the diversity of opinion to prescribed yes/no responses, and these are often to questions that demand much more complex answers. It is unavoidable that this path of disillusionment will not only prompt but further recycle *skepticism* and cynicism. Again, skepticism is a healthy reaction that people develop through experience and through thinking about processes deeply. Skeptics are not easily impressed. They are sometimes optimistic, sometimes pessimistic, and often neither. They are measured and invested. They may have been disappointed in the past, but they still care. Cynics, I believe, have surrendered, and it is this absence of hope that concerns me because it minimizes the potential for change.

My takeaway point from the assemblage of responses to the question of democracy is that we lack a contemporary vocabulary to describe it with. We use words of the past and retrofit them to new habits, in ways that leave us unfulfilled. Furthermore, we employ civic avenues of the past and repeat old habits, in ways that render us civically disinterested. This was the starting point of the second question I posed to my respondents, that of citizenship. I mentioned earlier that uncertainty was the feeling that permeated the conversation when respondents sought to define what democracy is. When they were asked what it means to be a citizen, responses typically led to an emotional finale of helplessness.

The starting point was, by all means, aspirational and hopeful. People have not given up on exercising their civic duties. There is *nobility* at the heart of the contemporary citizen, and unfortunately, it has not been tapped yet. People want to serve, want to help, and want to make the world better. No one starts from a point of doing wrong, although, often, one finds oneself out of options. That was where the helplessness seeped in, as citizens talked about the desire to contribute but the lack of avenues available for doing so. And so I began thinking about the *invisible citizen*, a citizen summoned to vote and then abandoned, a citizen wanting to speak but not listened to, a citizen looking to contribute to the local community and finding that one's efforts are undervalued and not counted as civic duty. People are playful, inspired, and fighters by nature. We have survival instincts, and those traverse all plains of our existence. But we increasingly find ourselves consumed by professional and personal obligations, saturated with information, and out of time to be political. Further, we are presented with opportunities for engaging with others that are boring, for lack of a better word. They are no longer exciting because they belong to a world of the past. They have ceased to energize us because we have been practicing them for centuries, and naturally, we would like something up to date, new civic habits. Politics does not have to be boring, yet the formulas we are taught for being political often reproduce routines that we no longer find rewarding.

Indeed, the people I spoke with found inspiration in micro-activities in their communities, because that is where they were afforded the autonomy to be political in their own way. They were able to interact with others in lively and imaginative ways, and they felt the direct and fairly immediate impact of their actions. If we want lively citizens, we have to offer engaging opportunities of interaction. And this is what I take with me as I look at the key themes that emerged when I asked people what was wrong with democracy and what might become better.

The defining mood that drove this part of the conversation was indisputably indignation. *Populism, corruption*, and the lack of *education* emerged as core themes and problems of democracy. People have no problem in identifying what is wrong with democracy, but they also have no means to fix it. And they have become tired of seeing the same problems surface time and time again, through different historical iterations. Older adults are more patient as they talk with me, and as I look into their eyes, I see wisdom, experience, and hope. They have seen this scenario play out before, and they have coping mechanisms for dealing with it. Midlife adults are annoyed and bewildered; they are the ones who tend to give me the most specific recommendations for how to fix things. Young adults are indignant, impatient, and passionate, and they give me the most original and idealistic responses. This fills me with hope. If our most experienced citizens are wise enough to teach us patience, then we can use time to our benefit. If our citizens who have seen something but not everything are still producing specific ideas, then we can use brain power to our benefit. Finally, if our young citizens are passionate and original, then we have the imagination needed to rethink all this. In other words, we have it in us to drive change throughout our life course and at different points of our life course.

Strikingly, very few of my participants mention technology as the problem. It is sometimes referenced as part of the problem, but again the core issues are identified as corruption, populism, and education. *Corruption* is framed as capitalism that is working against and not for democratic ideals. *Populism* is defined as an affective drive of inflated and unmet promises, often amplified through media. And *education* is identified as something that is absent among politicians. Even though citizens recognize that greater levels of literacy would help them sift through the information they receive daily in a more knowing manner, they point the finger at politicians as being civically ill equipped to do their jobs, as lacking the educational background required to fulfill their duties. They will vote politicians into office because we all have to vote for someone. Yet, while I conversed with citizens of diverse ideological orientations, I met no citizen who was excited by or admired their elected officials.

Ten Ways Forward

So what is democracy? Silence and noise. Ambivalence and familiarity. Equality. Voice. Skepticism. What is citizenship? Some variety of civic nobility that is unfortunately rendered invisible by our civic radars. How can we make democracy better? By fixing things we have always failed at: corruption, populism, and education. What has technology done so far? Mostly amplified these tendencies, in ways that have not yet permitted us to give democracy the tune-up that it so clearly needs. Here are some suggestions that emerge out of the citizen narratives.

1. *Reverse the Trend: Soft Capitalism and Strong Democracy*

Citizens understand that money drives politics. This interferes with democracy. Every interview I conducted included discussions about the connection between capital and governance and the detrimental effect this has on the democratic process. Whether my participants were left or right leaning, progressive or conservative, young or old, from Russia or from Canada, the bottom line was this: special interests, representing a financial advantage for the select few, exert a considerable influence on politics. Capitalism is strong and ubiquitous. It is globalized, so it even influences the priorities of non-capitalist countries. There is no way to opt out of it. It lies at the heart of what people term corruption when they identify core problems in democracies. People are concerned that when the motivation to raise capital is prioritized, democratic initiatives suffer.

Let's not pretend that capitalism will be replaced by a better economic system. Capitalism excels at generating income, fails at distributing it equally. Because competition drives capitalism, by definition rewards are competitively allocated and thus not on an equal basis. Capitalism is a system of financial management, not of political governance. Democracy is a system of governance, not of financial management. We are presently at a stage where capitalism is strong and influences the processes of governance. The trend needs to be reversed so that there is a balance between the system of finance and the system of governance. At present, we need to set processes in place that allow us to promote softer models of capitalism that set the stage for stronger democracies.

There is no recipe for soft capitalism that works for all countries. Each context calls for its own solution. What the frequent cycles of financial upturn and downturn that we seem to have experienced with greater frequency over the past thirty years show, however, is that there is a level of financial uncertainty that is part of how capitalism operates today. When this uncertainty turns into financial insecurity for the average citizen, the effect spills over into how people behave, live, and vote.[1] History has taught us that populism reaches a peak during times of financial insecurity. Several economists and social scientists have suggested corrective mechanisms that permit markets to work competitively yet ensure financial stability for the greater public too.[2] Softening capitalism is not an impossibility, nor is it an act that renders capitalism ineffective. It is a message that economists have been writing about and that billionaires have also advocated for, through offering a variety of solutions and options.

We run twenty-first-century societies on an economic model that emerged in the early Renaissance—some would argue even a little earlier. It is time for some revisions to the model, so that the form of capitalism does not define the form of politics. I am reminded of what one of my informants from the United Kingdom, Aristotle (moniker selected by him, once I told him the project was about democracy), a former executive officer at Goldman Sachs, told me: "We take many steps to regulate oligopolies and ensure monopolies do not dominate the market. Why do we allow monopolies to exist in democracies?" He was referring, of course, to the bipartisan politics that tend to define the political spectrum in most countries. These bipartisan politics are a side effect of capitalist mechanisms of funding parties. We encounter them more frequently in countries that require their candidates to raise their own funds for campaigning, such as the United States. "Any system that only has two parties is not really a democracy," adds Nathan, from Canada. Indeed, the lack of difference between the solutions that political candidates offer frequently renders a civic monopoly that leaves citizens wanting more options. The core elements of stout capitalism already influence the form that civic options take in contemporary democracies. By reversing the trend, we can pave the way for softer capitalism and more pluralistic democracy.

2. *Micro-governance*

The more I spoke with people around the world, the more aware I became of how fulfilling they found tiny acts of civic participation in their own communities. From those who volunteered at election centers to people who never engaged in any form of organized volunteerism, people became most civically enthralled when they spoke about initiatives taking place in their own neighborhoods, communities, towns, cities, and regions. When the discussion moved to forms of central governance, they became distant and detached. The tone of conversation became more cynical, and people spoke with uncertainty about the outcomes of policy that came out of centrally located governance. There was a disconnect between micro- and macro-governance, which manifested itself in two ways. First, people tended to experience the majority of activities occurring on the micro level as impactful and fulfilling. By contrast, they internalized the majority of activities occurring on the macro level as non-impactful and had trouble pointing to specific government policies that they identified as meaningful. "You know what," VC, interviewed in Greece, told me with a poignant smile, "most of the accomplishments in the arts and sciences that we admire, the monuments that we go visit as tourists, . . . those were not put into place by democracies."

It would be unfair to read this statement as a call for enlightened monarchs to take over. It certainly shows, however, that democratic leadership is not consistently perceived as enlightened. It further suggests that meso-mechanisms in place, be they government or media related, are not adequately connecting micro-communities to macro systems of governance located in large urban centers.

This is not a simple matter to be described as an urban-rural divide, although it certainly contains elements of that. City residents looked for micro-communities within the city and showed a preference for the elements of direct democracy they found there and indifference for the elements of representative democracy at work elsewhere. If, as I said earlier, democracy is a system that works best within micro-communities that are able to support direct, immediate, and reciprocal communication, then perhaps our efforts are best directed at strengthening those micro-communities and doing a better job of connecting them to larger systems of governance.[3] One might ask, Isn't this how the federal system of governance in the United States was designed to work? Indeed, it was, but at the time it was designed, the federally connected states were smaller, in size of population, economy, townships, organizations, and infrastructure. They were micro then; they no longer are now. Similarly, the European Union system was designed to connect nations that have since evolved beyond their geographic boundaries. So although the general principle works, the world has changed, and we need to adjust how we implement these principles. Our world has grown, and we run it with systems of governance that were built for different types of societies. Or perhaps, as Nathan from Canada told me, we have not "really tried these systems as they are idealized, as they should be yet."

3. *Counting Absence*

During my travels, I was struck by the following contradiction. Almost all of my interviewees emphasized the need to vote, frequently adding that if one does not vote, one does not have the right to complain. Yet at the same time, all my respondents experienced difficulty performing the task of voting, because they never seemed to be satisfied with the candidates they voted for. On the contrary, many reported often having to vote for the least worst option. As societies, we encourage voting, and we complain when voter turnout is low. It is not socially desirable to admit to not voting, and those who openly state that they did not vote are often chastised and encouraged to be more engaged. There is a paradox inherent in the behavior. We reward voting, even if it is to endorse candidates we do not deem qualified. We discourage not voting, even though that is because the selection of candidates is inadequate. Absence is counted as apathy. The act of not voting is read as disinterest. It strikes me that this is not an accurate reading. "To vote but also to not be pressured to vote" is how Nancy, from Canada, defines voting. Anna, a fellow Canadian, further explains that being a citizen should extend beyond "vote and recycle."

Absence is not always apathy. Absence occurs when there is no interest in the options offered. People do not refuse to vote because they are lazy. They refuse to vote because they do not believe doing so will make a difference. And yet nonvoters receive virtual demerit points in civic engagement. We render a disservice to those citizens when we count their nonvote as an act of indifference. Similarly, we assign a greater weight to the votes of those who selected from a pool of candidates regardless of how qualified they found those candidates to be. We thus penalize those who did not vote for having the courage to admit that none of the proposed options worked for them. We then reward those who selected the least worst option and, in so doing, inadvertently played a part in reproducing a cycle of mediocre candidates.

I am not suggesting that we do not show up to vote, but imagine what would happen if we did? Would that not send a strong message to politicians that they need to do better? The present system of voting is biased to reward the endorsement of candidates disproportionately by not counting absence as a rejection of candidates. A nonvote may be a signal of indifference, and it may also be a rejection of all the options offered. Until we afford citizens the opportunity to reject the choices and request new options, we will not have a voting system that provides an accurate read of voter sentiment. We are counting the registered voices and discounting the absent ones.

Silence does not always reflect the absence of opinion. Silence also reflects the need to ponder, study, and listen. These practices are the root of democracy, and we must find ways to reward them.[4] We are not allowing ourselves to listen to those who are staying quiet. We need to better understand the meaning of that silence. Then we must figure a way to count it as part of our democratic process.

4. *Long-Term and Short-Term Politics*

"Democracy is restricted temporally—which makes it very focused on the now, so it is very difficult to focus on larger issues. . . . We need a type of democracy that is accountable not just to the present but the future," says Anna, from Canada. I ponder this comment as I think about issues that concern the planet, including climate change, medicine, poverty, education, and peace. In our everyday lives, we plan for the long term and the short term. Families plan savings for the long term, to account for children's education, retirement, and other needs, and they also plan for the short term, to account for monthly or annual expenses. They make these decisions based on shared consensus about a number of things including where they are going to live, how and where they are going to work, where children may go to school, vacation planning, and general spending priorities. Similarly, organizations have short- and long-term growth plans, based on executive consensus on the past, present, and future trends and expectations. We plan for the short term and the long term and often for the interim. The only realm of our lives where long- versus short-term planning does not come into play is the political one, as Ayn, who lives in London and works for a consulting firm, reminds me.

Governments are voted into power on the basis of a set of promises executable on a four- or five-year plan. Several of these promises require structural changes that will take longer than that to put into effect, but neither we nor our media seem to question that. Governments are voted out of power, and the progress that had been made toward these goals is stalled. And when new governments are formed, they have the freedom to bow out of commitments that concern global priorities like climate change, supported by indisputable scientific data. These priorities do not appear to align with special interests, and this is where a touch of soft capitalism, mentioned earlier, would help. Democracies cycle through governments that do not have the time or leeway to follow through on their promises, as societies begin to look like assemblages of unfinished projects. Global consensus on long-term planning, enforced locally, ensures that progress is made on issues that are collectively deemed important. Short-term planning through various iterations of micro-governance would help address issues of regional relevance in a manner that is satisfying for citizens.

5. *Beyond Voting*

Annett, an eighty-four-year-old retired retailer from Germany, finds that levels of participation in politics have increased over time, especially at the local level. She finds hope in the engagement that demonstrations and referenda (including the reactions to them) draw from people. Thomas, a technology consultant living in London, on the other hand, insists that if referenda must be used, they move beyond simplistic binary options. These are just a couple of many reactions I recorded as I talked with people about the things that excite them about democracy and the times when they are let down. These reactions come up when we talk about what it means to be a citizen, and they often are offered as solutions when we discuss what is wrong with democracy. Here is one practice that does not seem to excite people at all: voting. All participants appreciate the right to vote and see it as part of their civic duty. At the same time, they have come to view it as an obligatory beginning of their civic journey and one that often involves them being counted but not feeling like they are counted, as the political scientist Stephen Coleman has eloquently argued.[5]

This is precisely the point: we look at voting as the penultimate point of civic engagement for citizens. This is because, for many years, many of us did not have the right to vote and had to fight to earn it. That does not mean, however, that it is the final step. On the contrary, it should be understood as the inaugural point of formal civic engagement. Voting is how we vote governments in. The fact that we have been given the power to vote governments in but we do not have the power to vote them out seems imbalanced. Governments can be voted out either through our elected representatives or when we are called in to vote a new government in. It would not be unreasonable to have avenues for voting out or formally registering disagreement with the direction a government takes. Several countries do have midterm elections, and those are often used to signal endorsement or lack thereof of governments in place. Still, these do not offer mechanisms for replacing democratically elected systems that have let citizens down. We resort to protesting, petition signing, and contacting our representatives, hoping that they will listen, and thus get caught up in a never ending cycle of cynicism as the responses we receive are never adequate. I realize that this idea may be perceived as extreme and may be complicated to enforce. It could also potentially introduce more problems than it would solve if it were exploited. I bring it up, however, to point at an imbalance in participation that can be corrected through a variety of measures. We have a system in place that forces politicians to court citizens for their vote around election time. Yet citizens are more than mere votes to be lured. They trust politicians with their votes, and we should consider mechanisms for revoking that trust when the bond has been broken.

In the past, we have often used polling as a way of gauging public opinion. The election cycles of the past few years have effectively revealed how polling can be manipulated, how it can be affected by mis- or disinformation, and importantly, how it can misrepresent what the public wants. Scholars have long described the reasons why polling does not work for contemporary democracies. In the early chapters of this book, I discussed the way polling interferes with the electoral process, by confining responses to predetermined options, by removing the option for silence, and by taking away the right to choose which question we respond to and the form these questions take. Once again, we are using instruments that we have outgrown and tools that undermine our civic agency, and the effect is the same as trying to fit into old clothes that no longer work for our bodies, our personalities, and our lives. Let's create new civic avenues for participation, and let's use technology or design new technology that can help us pave those avenues. An example of soft capitalism at work would involve software companies that design with democracy as a goal, not an afterthought. Yet another example of soft capitalism at work would release candidates in countries like the United States from the burden of a drawn-out election period, one that forces them to play to the economics of media attention and raise enough funds to stay in a campaign race that lasts nearly two years. Voting processes that no longer work can be revised, with long-term planning in mind and agreement across all parties and publics, so that changes are not abandoned halfway. Finally, to politicians who have always struggled with the internet: it is not a tool for you to speak to your constituents. That is better done in person and can be effected through forms of micro-governance that I have previously discussed. People are too cynical about the media to trust politicians through them. The internet and the platforms that it supports are there to provide a way for politicians to listen to the nuanced conversations people have online, the ones that do not fit into the prescribed categories of polling and referenda. Politicians should put their ears to the ether and listen.

6. *A Civic Education for All*

My respondents earnestly spoke with me about the need for education. They felt overwhelmed by the volume of information they received on a daily basis and were eager to find a way to read through it all so as to stay informed and civically engaged. Often, the more they read, the more they found themselves reading about the same things over and over again. They spoke about wanting to read about what happened rather than having to read someone's opinion about what happened instead. They explained that their own personal and professional obligations left them with little time to keep up with what is happening around the world. In chapter 3, I wrote in great detail about the changing rhythms of our everyday lives and how incompatible they are with our civic obligations. It is obvious that journalistic media are not catering to the needs of citizens in a manner that is gratifying. Furthermore, it becomes apparent that citizens seek a number of things out in their information environments, and these include opportunities for enlightenment as well as diversion.

Beyond personal concerns, however, the people I conversed with worried that their own politicians lacked basic education in civics and in public affairs to perform their own jobs. This, of course, begs the question of why, if that is the case, they were ever voted into office; and the answer is that people are not presented with the options that they want. Regardless, politics appears to be the only realm that people may enter and advance in with an absence of experience. An absence of experience in governance is often greeted as a mark of authenticity, whereas a number of years in governance are read as a sure sign of corruption. And so, while we interview for jobs and are awarded them on the basis of skills and experience, we frequently judge political candidates on how they present themselves. Do they seem authentic? Do they look like someone we might have a beer with? Are they speaking in relatable terms? As a result, those who do well in this mediated process through which we interview candidates are those who are media savvy and not necessarily those who are the most well versed. There are exceptions to this rule, of course. But for change to occur, we have to hold politicians to the same high standards that are applied to us. We are not selecting actors to play the part. While politicians must be immediate and relatable, that is one of many qualities they should possess, and most of my participants found them lacking in those areas. Send them to school, some of my informants exclaimed.

Although sending politicians to school or requiring a certain level of education for them creates barriers to entry for democratic governance that we want to avoid, requiring a minimum level of knowledge is not unreasonable. Without favoring elites who have had the privilege of a better education, we might create a system that ensures that both pre- and post-election, all elected officials are educated on short- and long-term issues. And with that, we must train our own eyes and ears to look beyond the surface and our own biases to the substance of each candidate we evaluate.

7. *Forget Messiahs*

Most politicians are uncomfortable with the manner in which media like radio, TV, and photojournalism blur public and private boundaries. Joshua Meyrowitz, a scholar of media and political communication, captures this best in his award-winning classic *No Sense of Place*. Meyrowitz argues that modern media alter the situational geography of everyday life.[6] These media blur public and private boundaries, leaving many of us, and politicians especially, confused about which behaviors are best suited for public spaces and which work best in private. Most importantly, however, modern media invite immediacy in a way that lifts a preexisting veil of secrecy between politicians and citizens. This is not necessarily detrimental to public life, for it demystifies politics for many of us. Still, it encourages politicians to self-present in a way that makes them as approachable as the person next door. Since politicians must be relatable to millions, the task of being everyone's next-door neighbor becomes impossible. Therefore, they end up developing different personas or "faces" that they present, depending on the situation they find themselves in. This is a reasonable response and an everyday practice for all of us. We have a certain persona for work, a different demeanor at home with family, and yet another sense of character with friends. Through our everyday interactions, we seek to maintain continuity, but as we traverse spaces that are public, private, or a little bit of both, we find that we need to adjust our behaviors in order to remain true to who we are and who we aspire to be.

When politicians engage in a similar modification of behavior through media, however, it reads as inauthentic. The illusion of proximity that modern media offer forces politicians to put on a performance that is often incompatible with their personalities. Richard Nixon allegedly lost the televised debates and eventually the U.S. presidential election to John F. Kennedy in part because he refused to wear makeup on TV back in the 1960s. What would be read as a deeply authentic gesture to remain true to himself and appear as he was resulted in him looking darker, tired, and sweaty, all qualities that led the public to believe that he was not trustworthy. Kennedy, on the other hand, while not strikingly more eloquent than his opponent in that debate, had agreed to wear makeup and was able to present a demeanor that read as respectable and confident on TV. Politicians operate somewhere between public and private space when they use media, in a manner that robs all of us of what Meyrowitz calls a sense of place, a situational definition of the context that drives their actions.

We look for politicians who are trustworthy and relatable, but we do not realize that media operate in ways that often require people to *play a part in order to appear to be themselves.* Kennedy played himself successfully on TV because he effectively used props that were at hand. It is uncertain that he would survive the greater overlap between public and private spheres that social media introduce today. Leaders often appear as great orators on TV, but we forget that they employ speechwriters and that much of their rhetorical success relies on performance: Reagan's steady tone, Clinton's slight nod to the right, Blair's reassuring tone, even Obama's deliberate monotone that affirmed him as authentic. We forget to realize that it is not humanly possible for someone to be a capable leader of a country and act like our next-door neighbor. There is a reason why our next-door neighbor is not running for office, after all.

Social media further amplify the overlap between public and private spheres, leaving politicians at a loss when it comes to making use of social media. Most of them use social media to talk at people, which leaves the public deeply disappointed. Some attempt to use social media to converse with people, which is challenging, given the nature of these media. It is unreasonable to expect someone to carry on coherent asynchronous conversations with millions of people and run a country at the same time. Finally, politicians are human beings, who, like all of us, have a private life. I am deeply suspicious these days of anyone who is effortlessly comfortable with using social media, with blurring private and public, with openly sharing details of their private life, with parading their families and young children on televisions as part of an electoral campaign. I am disturbed that it has become the norm that politicians appear publicly, that is, through media, surrounded by their families, as a way of asserting normalcy, as a way of showing that they are just like us. We should vote them into office because we perceive them to be better than us. And we are voting them, not their spouses or significant others or children, into office, so there is no reason for political families to enter our civic landscape.

Now, let me take this point to its natural climax by talking about a particular breed of politician who is quite comfortable setting one foot in the private sphere and the other in the public sphere and performing a persona that draws crowds in support: the so-called messiah.

Messiahs are comfortable with the overlap of public and private and are adept at using social media not just as their personal PR agents but also as a way to energize publics that they connect with and publics that they aggravate—that they annoy. In true populist fashion, they promise to solve problems but do not offer specific details.[7] President Trump is skilled at using social media. His tweets are not directed at his allies and supporters; it is well known that he interacts with them in person at rallies or through dedicated media that are reliable followers of the president. His tweets are directed at the media and his opponents, and they serve as a successful distraction from the events of the day. It takes zero time for the media to forget the situational context and get caught in the game of repeating, commenting on, and further amplifying the president's point of view. President Trump has mastered this rhetorical strategy of distraction, but he is not the only one. Former prime minister Alexis Tsipras of Greece, voted out of office in 2019 after involvement in numerous scandals, had a practice of swaying crowds through speeches delivered in public squares or televised appearances. Boris Johnson and Nigel Farage, the architects of Brexit, employed a similar rhetoric of distraction, online and offline, that centered around Brexit refrains and avoided much specificity. The promise that is commonly delivered by messiahs is that of resurrection. Messiahs present as saviors, who make problems go away. They are never specific, and the loss of contextual definition that modern media encourage allows them to thrive.

8. Game the System: News Media, Headlines, and the Economics of Attention

News headlines introduce, frame, and contextualize.[8] They award significance, communicate gravitas, and reinforce status. They inform and misinform. They are a crucial part of how news turns into a story. In the long term, they play a part in how stories are retold and recorded, thus eventually turning into memories and histories. In the short term, they organize the economics of attention. In contemporary societies, where information is a commodity, the economics of attention reign supreme. Imagine now the headline, repeated, through a variety of media but with no story below it—a headline that is designed to attract your attention, for the purpose of directing you to a particular website, feed, or program. Much of the contemporary structure of news storytelling uses arresting headlines, or clickbait, to serve up stories of arguable substance. My conversations often revealed disappointment in the lack of in-depth coverage of the issues that matter.

Let me now explain the effect of a news infoscape that is dominated by headlines, presented in the form of news scrollers, retweets, and refrains that appear at regular intervals across your screens. The presentation of headlines may have changed over time, but the form remains the same. The language is meant to be short, summary, and sharp. The words bring the crucial elements of the story to the forefront, and the grammar and syntax drum up intensity, if needed. The verbal economy of headlines is tight, and it must work quickly and efficiently. It is meant to capture the attention of the reader without, ideally, compromising the essence of the story. Headlines not only lure but also direct the attention of the reader, and in doing so, they frame a story. They offer a lens through which to understand it. They kick-start the cognitive process. They frame the issue at hand, by selecting "some aspects of a perceived reality [to] make them more salient in a communicating text, in such a way as to promote a particular problem definition, causal interpretation, moral evaluation, and/or treatment recommendation."[9] Framing is guided by news values that prioritize recency, urgency, and proximity; the economy and political affairs; and privileged nations and dominant ideologies, while also appealing to viewers by being commonsensical, entertaining, and dramatic.[10] News values are about turning events into stories, and headlines present the first step in doing so.

Newer technologies do not radically reorganize how headlines are framed and which news values guide the framing process. But they do amplify visibility and pluralize access. Therefore, a directional lens offered through a frame becomes more visible, by reaching greater audiences more quickly. And in following suit with the ascent of the 24/7 news cycle that TV ushered in, new media platforms reinforce and reproduce an obsession with instantaneity in news reporting. Headlines must always be current. Headlines can now be revised without waiting for the next day's edition, so they are. Because they can be revised, they are constantly revised, lest the attention of readers drifts off. And so we live in a news ecology of the ever changing, always updateable news beat, headlines that are always already new.[11]

As a result, headlines become clickbait for a broad variety of news organizations, used to attract eyeballs. Hashtags become headlines, and tweets are reported as both the headline and the story. Headlines are algorithmically generated and propagated by bots, leading to news, actual or fake. Importantly, newer platforms afford anyone the opportunity to craft a headline and subsequently a news story. While this pluralizes the news ecology, it does not necessarily democratize the process. Actors, engaging in independent or coordinated acts of journalism, have a say in what story is told and how it is introduced to the public arena. We might understand this process as a form of networked framing and gatekeeping, in which a variety of actors, human and non-human, work together or on their own to crowd-source news content to prominence, via the use of conversational, social, and digitally enabled practices that symbiotically connect elite and crowd in framing what is relevant.[12] Technology is not neutral; it augments exposure. But it also does not discern between truth and fiction. Citizens, journalists, and politicians can.

Headlines are part of the allure of news reading. In the early days of newspapers, newsboys yelled them out to attract passersby. When newspapers were not affordable or accessible to all, headlines would form the basis for conversation as people gathered and read them in cafés. From the food trucks of New York City that displayed newspapers above the fold among coffees and hot dogs to the kiosks of Europe and South America with newspapers attached to a wire with clothespins, people would gather around, peruse the day's headlines, and engage in casual social conversation with one another. There is a cognitive element to how we process the news, and framing addresses how the cognitive process is engaged. But there is a soft drama to the process of reading the news, which is always engulfed in our everyday routine, whether that involves reading the newspaper in print form or browsing through a news site on one's phone on the train to work. There is emotion involved in how we approach and become entranced by the process of following the news; this is both a social and information-seeking process. And it is a process called into being via headlines. The affect of headlines, that is, the mood, the atmosphere, the feelings headlines evoke, both draws us in and further moves us emotionally. It lulls us into an environment where we become accustomed to discussing the headline, commenting on it, making jokes about it with friends, but rarely digging beneath the surface, because the headline, so often, *becomes the story*.

How do newer platforms reorganize the news experience? They fold into and further extend the effect of the twenty-four-hour news cycle and thus further cultivate and reproduce a fixation with instantaneity in news reporting. There are multiple ways in which digital and networked platforms of news storytelling amplify the prevalence of headlines, and I have referred to some in the preceding section. Here I want to focus on how technology lends texture to our affective reaction to the news. One key term in doing so is "premediation," which describes the form events take on *before* they turn into stories. Premediation is thus connected to processes of events in the making, to anticipating what the news is going to be like, to thinking about how the headline is going to read. Richard Grusin makes the point that premediation has dominated news storytelling post-9/11, a time when many of us, including news organizations, were struggling to make sense of what happened. He points to the news scroller, which became a staple of news storytelling during that time, as an example of this anticipation of the new, conveyed through the anxiety of constantly updating headlines.[13] The form of the news scroller has dictated the stylistic and visual presentation of news online. It is a form that induces anticipation and, with that, anxiety, a state of always expecting the new.

Elsewhere, I have described this form of news storytelling as affective news.[14] It is not a form of news storytelling that invites cool reflection, thoughtful fact-checking, and in general, slow news. Affective news is native to ambient, always-on architectures that utilize a variety of social media, including Twitter, Facebook, and Reddit in particular. Affective reactions are not news, nor are they headlines. They stem out of social experiences of reading the news and are typically phatic, spontaneous reactions to reading a story. They are our primary way of responding to a story and eventually evolve into a more nuanced opinion. Problems arise when affect, or an affective reaction, becomes the story. And so instead of news, we get mere headlines, repeated to the rhythm of the news scroller, our social media feeds, constant news updates, and always-breaking news. When headlines are repeated affectively, with no follow-up story or context, then we hear a lot about Secretary of State Hillary Clinton's emails without ever finding out exactly what happened. We constantly receive news alerts about President Trump not making his tax returns available, but we are spared the specifics of how this is possible or what those tax returns would reveal. We become alarmed about Brexit, but we never manage to learn about the complexities that led to that particular development. In other words, we get intensity but no substance.

The economics of attention has never been absent from the business of news storytelling. Headlines are central to the economics of attention, as they are the lead mechanism of drawing in readers. Assuming that this is a new problem, or even a problem, is devoid of any understanding of the business of news making and the ways in which decisions are made in the newsroom. Headlines must work in a way that is financially viable for the news storytelling business. News is a business, and the people who are tasked with reporting the news function in the market economy of news making. The business of news making exists inside the scope of late capitalism and operates within its confines, in order to be financially sustainable. Reconciling economics with the politics of truth telling is no easy task and has always complicated life for journalists and news organizations. These difficulties are not insurmountable, but they require maintaining a delicate balance in the newsroom, a task that frequently falls to editors who must be clever and resourceful.

Social media do not simplify this equation at all. On the contrary, because newspapers are in the business of selling information and newer media make sharing information exceptionally easy, social media platforms augment long-standing tensions of treating information as an economic good. Information is an abstraction. Unlike other commodities that are bought and sold in economic markets, information does not possess a tangible material basis. So do a lot of services, but what makes information unique as a commodity is its abstract nature. Information cannot be sold, produced, or distributed in distinct units. Unlike other goods, it cannot be completely used up or consumed. Even when sold, it still remains with the producer. Most important, it is valued differently by each potential customer. For all these reasons, information remains an elusive commodity; it wants to be free. It remains a subjectively defined entity with a particular kind of lightness that makes it difficult to trade.

For networked, globally active or locally specific news organizations, information is a key variable to prosperity and growth. But failure to realize that information is ultimately an abstraction, and not a commodity, frequently leads to efforts to compartmentalize information and sell it in bits or bytes, package it in the form of lists and clickbait content, and auction off its most attention-grabbing elements, even though those are often not the most valuable ones. There is no easy way out of this conundrum. Change takes patience and cooperation. It would require, first, that leading news institutions come to an accord on the market principles that will define the news economy and, second, that news institutions become partially or wholly financially independent. There is historical precedent for news organizations joining forces during times of crisis, so while difficult, the task at hand is not impossible.[15]

9. Reinvent Journalism

Newer media technologies afford innovative ways for news storytelling that may go a long way toward reconnecting politicians and the media with a disaffected public. Unfortunately, they are typically co-opted into conventional economics of production, thus producing clickbait headlines, bot-friendly leads, and drama-inducing angles. These tendencies and tensions further augment tensions in the chasm that Hannah Arendt identified between truth and politics. They reached a climax in the most recent electoral cycles and during the period this book was being researched, but they are certainly not new. So what do we do about the tensions between journalism, politicians, and publics?

In a sense, journalism has always been in crisis, a crisis brought on by the difficulty of reconciling the necessities of truth telling with the priorities of politics. Journalists are the ones confronted with this almost impossible task daily, and newer media both amplify its magnitude and offer a way out: literacy. Above all, networked platforms offer opportunities for connection and expression. They afford openings to reach out to others to fight, troll, and converse and also to listen, learn, and educate (oneself and others). Ultimately, the surest safeguard is critical literacy; it is learning to look beyond headlines and search for the story.

A number of years ago I embarked on a line of research that was designed to understand how Twitter functions as a news storytelling platform. This was around 2010. Twitter was a different medium then, and it supported mostly community-oriented conversation among friends with some snark, a peculiar blend of mass broadcast polyphonic communication that emerged out of mostly one-to-one, dyadic conversations. There was a lot of speculation about how news organizations might use it and also about how citizens could put it to work. And then came the Arab Spring, spreading through the Middle East and North Africa, and the Indignados movement in Spain, and Occupy in the United States. These movements showed us the part that Twitter could play in helping to tell the stories of movements that media institutions were not prepared to understand.

There was a lot of talk back then about whether social media, mainly Twitter, made the revolutions. That was a useless conversation. Change is gradual. Revolutions are long. They have to be long, in order to attain meaning. And sometimes they lead away from and not toward democracy, as we have seen. So, no, social media do not make or break revolutions. But those revolutions definitely made social media. In so doing, they reinforced this brand of news that I call affective. And this brand of news enables messiahs of all sorts, political and not.

What is affective news? It emerged as we studied the crowd-sourced, bottom-up, live-tweeted, curated, swarm-fact-checked stream of news that took over news storytelling during the Arab Spring and many of the movements that followed it. Affective news is a mix of live-tweeted news reports, drama, fact, and opinion blended into one, to the point where discerning one from the other is not possible and doing so misses the point. It is not new, but it is amplified by social media. What is "affect," and why do I term this brand of news "affective"?

"Affect" is not the same as "emotion." These were not emotional news reports we were reading. "Affect" is the sensation you feel before you experience an emotion and before your cognitive mechanisms kick in and help you label that feeling as an emotion.

When you tap your foot to a song you like, that is an affective reaction. When you hum a song you enjoy, that is an affective reaction.

What does affective news look like? Well, short, report-like, with some opinion and drama thrown in, in less than about two hundred characters, and above all intense. Affect is not feeling. It is about the intensity with which we feel. It is the difference between my poking you and my pushing you or shoving you to the ground. It is the difference between a caress to the cheek and a slap to the face—same gesture, but different intensity, revealing different intentions and a different outcome. How does this idea connect to messiahs?

Messiahs connect affectively. They present that mix of "facts," drama, opinion, and intensity blended into one. The problem is that not only do they deliver that, but journalists pick up on it and are enamored by it, whether they agree with it or not. Or perhaps it is not journalists who are enamored by it but the attention economy that drives news. When has news not been driven by an attention economy? The bottom line is, this gets reported as news.

Thus, news media reproduce affective narratives. And here is the thing. Affect, intensity, is not an event. It is a way for citizens to sense their way through a story. Things become problematic when affect, this intensity, is reported *as* the event. In this manner, we observe tweets that automatically become headlines—with no fact-checking, no editorial acumen exercised. We hear one-liners filled with alarming intensity—but never receive more substance. We hear a lot about plans—but never more detail. These one-liners are repeated over and over again as refrains, as choruses, that lull us into agreement or indignation to the point where we produce affective reactions of our own. What are some examples of these? We mute the channel, turn the news off, block, take long-term leaves from our social media feeds.

Affect—this form of intensity—can be very successful in sustaining feelings of community. And these feelings of community can either reflexively drive a movement forward or entrap publics in a state of disengaged passivity—a lot of intensity but no movement. Imagine being caught up in an ongoing, never ending, ever evolving loop of intensity with no way out, no form of release. This is a nightmare for citizens. Yet it is the civic reality most of us around the world exist in. The civic infoscape of this reality is sustained by our media.

My recommendation for journalists is to evolve and to use technology to do so. Journalists make regular use of technology but typically to reproduce old habits and routines. The technology is there to afford people opportunities for expression and connection. Citizens use it to express opinions and to connect with others. Journalists should use the technology to listen to citizens, amplify their voices, and connect with them. It is only through repeated connective practices that journalists can begin to rebuild the trust that is lost as the media business becomes immersed in the economics of attention. News organizations can take advantage of the economics of attention and produce worthwhile stories. Profit and quality can coexist, and technology can help make that happen, rather than simply help with tracking activity or advertising. Technology can lower the cost of producing a story; it can be used to tell a story in more engaging terms and can be used to help track stories in disconnected urban or rural neighborhoods as well as far-off locations in the world. It can be used to allow citizens to view the story from the perspective of the journalist, thus paving the way to rebuilding that trust. The curation of trust will not happen instantaneously, nor is it possible to implement these practices immediately. Slow yet steady processes of change can help restore the public's lost faith in the media.

Journalists, in the so-called post-truth age, need to define truth, need to be truth finders. If people trust journalists, then journalists can connect them to politicians. Media can restore and repair the lost faith in politics if used right. Journalists can be democracy's conduits of trust and, in doing so, be agents of change.

Change. Evolve. Technology is not here to be molded into journalists' dominant paradigm but to help them reinvent it.

What do we do with messiahs? Refuse to elevate them to prominence. Treat them as humans, humans with faults and with talents. Find out what they are really like behind the messianic projection. Let's not afford messiahs a platform. Let's not amplify their voice, reproduce it online, provide them with ready access to platforms. Messiahs use media. That is how they attain messianic status. Without media, they are mere humans, often mediocre humans. With media, they present as saviors. Journalists must be, in the words of James Hamilton, democracy's detectives.[16] They are truth finders. They are not storytellers. They must resist the tyranny of the narrative, which forces us to come up with characters, drama, plot twists—they are truth finders who work with storytelling media.

10. *Be Our Own Civic Agents of Change*
Citizens, you are the storytellers. Tell stories to make sense of things, of who you are, how you fit into this world. In an attention economy, your attention is a powerful commodity. It's your path to agency. Choose how you focus your attention. Don't squander your attention on clickbait headlines. Your attention is your power.

No one is going to save us. Living in a democracy requires protecting others. *The democratic condition is a human condition.* It's not about politics or governance. It is about being human. We try. And we often make mistakes.

Candidates in elections are running to fulfill a position, a job. The campaign should be an interview process, not entertainment. Elections are when we decide between job candidates. We do not need a superhero to solve our problems for us. We need a qualified, experienced manager who believes in our shared vision, a vision that includes respecting long- and short-term goals that we have collaboratively agreed to.

Finally, let's reject the things we are not happy with. We have to communicate dissatisfaction first in order for others to understand that we are not happy. Let's break old habits that we don't find satisfying and create new ones. Avoid lulling ourselves into the rhythms of civic engagement that others are creating for us. Tune out of televised debates that give candidates sixty seconds to offer solutions to problems that have existed for centuries. Reject formats that you do not find fulfilling. Turn a deaf ear to civic conversations that divide candidates into winners and losers. Let's create an environment where a meaningful conversation is key, and let's teach ourselves, children, and those around us to talk in a noncompetitive manner. In prizing the art of conversation, let's reward practices that lead to consensus and steer our attention from deliberation that elects a winner and a loser. Democracy is not a boxing match. There are no winners and losers. There is consensus, and that is the driver of democracy. Let's refuse to order and consume from a menu of civic options that was not created for us or by us. Cultivate our lie detectors—how can we trust bots to help us sift through misinformation when our lie detectors are subpar? Strangers from around the world, use technology to connect, to express yourselves, and to listen. Yes, you have the right to an opinion, but have you earned it? Resist technologies that are designed to recycle old patterns. Reject them, often and consistently. Eventually, the message will be heard. Take charge of your everyday life and, in so doing, of your everyday democracy.

Technologies network us, yes. But it is our stories that connect us, identify us, and potentially disconnect us. Journalists can use technology to give us access to information of a better quality, equal access to that information, and information that is whole, not served up in broken-up narratives, attractive headlines, and fragments of stories. That way, we can tell the stories that identify us, bring us closer, and do not divide us, so we can be better civic adults and so we do not need messiahs. Finally, let's be persistent and patient, because change takes time. It needs to take time in order to lead to meaningful re-form. We have to get through democracy to get to what might follow democracy.

After Democracy

Any movement forward is defined by the vision that we develop for our collective future. It is not uncommon for our expectations to be divided between a dystopian and a utopian binary. The dramatized narratives that evolve out of such traditions of dualistic thinking trap us into understanding technology as either entirely detrimental to humanity's well-being or fundamentally responsible for our ability to survive what the future might bring. Compelling as the stories that emerge may be, they do little more than expose our deepest fears and hopes in a vernacular that makes it difficult to distinguish between the two. Still, if we are to imagine what might follow democracy and present a better system of governance for us, we must first confront and understand the roots of our insecurities and our aspirations.

I have outlined ten conditions that give form to tendencies and tensions that surround contemporary societies, whether democratic or not. In so doing, I have clarified that these ten suggestions must be implemented jointly to work. A softer yet functional capitalism is central in helping to rebuild relationships of trust that are broken in contemporary societies. Emerging forms of federally coordinated micro-governance would not only create more fulfilling civic micro-ecologies but help in creating pathways for socially responsible forms of capitalism to grow. Counting absence as abstinence from and not disinterest in civic duty would send a strong message to governments that are formed by a majority vote from a diminishing percentage of people making it to the voting booths. A majority vote produced by a society that has less than half of its citizens voting is not majority vote. Long- and short-term planning might reenergize voters who have become disillusioned when they have seen long-term policies on climate change, health care, security, diplomacy, international relations, and worldwide peace modified or abandoned as governments get voted out and new ones get voted in. New civic habits, cultivated around the lifestyles of the present and the future, would motivate voters and put to rest a tired civic culture that reinforces a horse-race mentality of winners and losers. There should be no winners or losers in the collaborative consensus that democracy is about. Media and digital literacy should help citizens, politicians, and the media read through the performance and prioritize the substance behind the messages they are receiving. Media organizations that function more as a non-profit and less as a conglomerate could become the enabling mechanism of a softer, socially responsible form of capitalism that is more fitting to the priorities of the twenty-first century. An infoscape that is premised on these principles would aid us all to feel more connected, counted, and included. Importantly, it would provide us with decision-making tools that let us forget about messiahs and elect people whose plan—not TV persona—we trust.

A Transhuman Democracy

This process of change will be slow and gradual and will require us to delve into territory that is unfamiliar. Still, it is necessary, because we are advancing to the next stage of political governance that will follow democracy, whether we like it or not. And getting there with unfinished business, unresolved problems, and a chronic misunderstanding of what democracy is about will not be tragic. The impact will not be catastrophic. We will survive. We somehow always do. What will be tragic is that we could be accomplishing so much more with the evolutionary steps we have made as a species, and yet we end up constraining ourselves because of our chronic misapplication of technology.

It is only natural that we seek to use technology to improve how we did things in our past. At the same time, we must resist this urge, because our technologies, of all varieties, are here to do more than create efficiency. They are meant to help us reimagine routines, so that they become more engaging, more fun, more inspiring, and eventually, because they are all those things, more efficient too. For example, the World Wide Web was not created so that newspapers could take their print version and make it available online as a way to lure readers. This was a critical mistake that many of us cautioned against, for we felt that it underestimated the potential of the internet. Still, it became the dominant practice and led to the cultivation of an environment where people expect to receive news online for free, revenues for newspapers have diminished, quality reporting cannot be supported financially, misinformation and disinformation thrive, and corrective mechanisms are difficult to enforce. On the contrary, the World Wide Web presented a wonderful opportunity for newspapers and journalists to connect with the public, to come up with more contemporary models of financing and running a newspaper, to make it easier for journalists to conduct truth-finding, and to provide avenues for rebuilding trust with the public that was already eroding.

What will the next cycle of political governance look like? Transhuman. It should not surprise us or scare us. It is unavoidable. All of the apps and interfaces that we use today did not exist a mere ten years ago. It is most probable that in the next ten years they will be replaced by devices that maximize applications of sensor fusion, quantum mechanics, nanotechnology, and advanced forms of what we have come to term artificial intelligence. AI is human-generated intelligence and is no more or less artificial than other forms of intelligence we produce with minds and bodies. Many of these technologies will have the capacity to be integrated with our environments, including our bodies. Some already are. This should be greeted not with alarm but with care. Because these technologies will eventually expand our capabilities as humans, they should be designed with the same principles and attention that we apply when we design prosthetics, artificial organs, and numerous other devices that enhance our capabilities to battle medical conditions.

The challenge is that several of the technologies will be ubiquitous to the point of invisibility. They will be everywhere and nowhere at the same time. They will blend in to our environments seamlessly in a way that renders them unnoticeable. They will not interrupt our daily routines but will discreetly repeat, reinforce, and enhance them. And therein lies the danger of using technology, once again, to repeat the habits, errors, tendencies, and tensions of the past. We are able to engineer and design our way out of a future that repeats the past. Doing so requires paying attention to the following three core conditions we have been casual about thus far.

First, as we become societies with unprecedented capacities to generate, record, and share data, we must become more cognizant of the data we produce and what those data mean for our everyday lives. Our present habits are paving the way for us becoming black-boxed societies, societies that are managed by algorithms generated by humans in ways that accidentally omit the human from the equation.[17] The irony embedded in the design of algorithms is that although they are designed to make data more accessible and thus visible, they inadvertently do so through concealing the mechanisms of data generation. As a result, various iterations of digital or data colonialism are enabled in ways that reinforce and reproduce patterns of social injustice.[18] As we augment mechanisms for quantifying data in the absence of mechanisms of enhancing the quality of those data, we run the risk of creating societies that are fueled on mediocre or low-quality data. To use a simple metaphor, if data are the new oil, imagine your engines running overtime on the most processed, cheaply produced, and low-quality fuel. Techno-colonialism is an inevitable outcome, as data are used to colonize or take control of certain cognitive, geopolitical, and culturally defined territories, creating new regimes of segregation between the haves and have-nots.[19] Data will always be a central part of how we run societies, democracy, and governance. What is essential is that we produce data that are humane and of good quality and that citizens are literate enough to read and see through the inadequacies of data effortlessly. We should be as apt at reading data as our ancestors were at picking a ripe tomato at the local market, finding solid land to build a settlement on, and determining which crops would grow on a given type of land.

Second, digital imperialism is a reality, and the only way to reimagine how we design technology is to part with it and minimize Western influence. Western hubs of technological innovation in the United States and Europe have long dominated the logic of how we design, price, and make technology available. These practices create a widening gap between Western and Eastern ways of doing and thinking and reinforce patterns of economic imperialism and injustice. Ever more important, however, they insulate our design ecology in a manner that renders our technology increasingly rigid and inflexible, when it should be strong yet gentle, soft yet smart, malleable and specific at the same time. If we want our societies to be more collaborative and collective, then we must offer technology that does more than create an app for collaboration; it must be technology designed from a collectivistic premise. We cannot think in a collective manner when our technologies are designed to highlight the individual. We retrofit Twitter, Facebook, Reddit, and other platforms to enhance collaboration, but this does not alter the fact that the infrastructure of these platforms rests on an individualistic premise. This becomes readily apparent when we compare these interfaces with those created in non-Western contexts. Indeed, if digital imperialism were less rampant, we would be likely to see greater diversity in non-Western design, as in order to stay profitable, a non-Western design now must compete with the West and thus must integrate some elements that are dominant in individualistic cultures. A number of years ago, I worked on an essay titled "What If the Internet Didn't Speak English?"[20] My co-author, Elaine Yuan, and I sketched out what an online environment might look like were it not dominated by the organizing principles and restrictions of the English language and a Western mentality and had acquired elements of the *strong and gentle* approach that permeates Eastern cultures. We think we afford ourselves an advantage by reproducing English-language media. We do not. We are limiting our options, our design ideas, and our collective futures.

Finally, our aesthetic when approaching technology should be informed by a symbiotic approach. If we are to advance to a trans-human state in a manner that does not threaten the essence of being human, our technologies must be sentient, yes, but we must be sentient also. We must embrace our sentiment and use it to en-hance our logic. We have long drawn false distinctions between reason and sentiment, our hearts and minds, our brains and our in-stincts. There is no point to distinctions that force us to do the im-possible: separate our heart from our mind. Those are connected in our bodies, and they are connected because they are meant to work together. What makes us human is our ability to integrate senti-ment and reason into acting. Coincidentally, this also makes us happier and more balanced. Whenever we fail to do so, we fail at being human. In perfecting sentience, we embrace our sentiment and use it to our advantage and not against our logic. We employ sentience to develop modes of communicating with others, human and non-, in ways that reimagine and expand, not just replicate, our existing senses. Transhuman democracy rendered through sentient ways and places of being will come after democracy.

So what next? To μέλλον αόρατον—that is, the future is not visi-ble, said the Greek rhetorician Isocrates, active in the fifth century BC, also known as the ancient Greek golden age. Isocrates always wanted to become a respected orator, but his low voice and rather tentative presence refocused his aspiration to teaching. He was so successful as a teacher that he is frequently referred to as one of the earliest self-help consultants, which is fitting, as part of the prescription here revolves around helping ourselves first in order to help democracy after.

We have no way of knowing what will follow. We do not have the agency to tell people what to do. I have presented ten ways forward so as to break on through to the next stage of democracy; these are not ten commandments. To be transhuman, we must be human first. To evolve out of modernity, we must be modern first—strong and gentle; Western and Eastern, to the point where it is difficult to discern one from the other; collectivist yet aware of our uniqueness at the same time. Evolve out of binaries, and exist, in the words of Jean Cocteau, in the center extreme. The future is uncertain, and there is no escaping the desire lines of democracy, past, present, and future.

Importantly, this book is about the sum of my conversations as they evolved beyond my own thoughts and preferences. I listened, and what I learned is that democracy lies within the individual. So as individuals, we must trust our senses and not fall prey to the fads of our times. Irony stripped the sincerity out of our democratic intentions. In order to reclaim itself, democracy must find its place first in each and every one of us, our bodies, our minds, our senses. Nothing is in the mind until it has first been in the sense, Thomas Aquinas famously said, so we must learn to interpret our senses, so that we can trust them and use them to move forward, synagonistically with our human and non-human fellows. Have conversations, not debates, with people who are interested in finding a way to agree and also with others who are vested in finding a way to disagree in a manner that is civil. Design technologies that reconsider what we do and for which democracy is not an afterthought but the driver. We have turned democracy into a rigid routine. We must use our imagination and trust our guts in learning to reinvent it. And we might then be able to traverse through and beyond it.

Unlearn the old habits.
Remember always; but also learn to forget.
Listen and then converse.
Look up, think in reverse, so as to move ahead.
Put this book away, rethink and reimagine.

Notes

ONE
What If?

1. Richard Sennett, *The Craftsman* (New Haven: Yale University Press, 2008).
2. Zizi Papacharissi, *Affective Publics: Sentiment, Technology, and Politics* (New York: Oxford University Press, 2015).
3. Zizi Papacharissi, "Affective Publics and Structures of Storytelling: Sentiment, Events and Mediality," *Information, Communication & Society* 19, no. 3 (2016): 307–324.
4. Stephan Coleman, *How Voters Feel* (Cambridge: Cambridge University Press, 2013).
5. Chantal Mouffe, *The Democratic Paradox* (London: Verso, 2000); Chantal Mouffe, *On the Political* (London: Routledge, 2005).
6. Zizi Papacharissi, *A Private Sphere: Democracy in a Digital Age* (Cambridge, U.K.: Polity, 2010).
7. For a brilliant take on what ensues when one asks *what if?* rather than *what is?* see my inspiration Svetlana Boym, *The Future of Nostalgia* (New York: Basic Books, 2001).
8. I have obtained IRB approval from my home institution, the University of Illinois at Chicago. Informants were provided with an information sheet that describes the study, translated as needed. I speak four languages and used translators as needed. Anonymity is guaranteed, and if quoted, informants had the opportunity to approve how they were quoted and elect pseudonyms they prefer to use. The University of Illinois system recently recognized me as University Scholar.

This is an honor reserved for productive scholars whose work has generated influence and comes with a monetary award of approximately $50,000. I used these funds for this project. Finally, I pilot-tested the questions with informants in Mexico City, Beijing, and Athens and found that it is easy to engage informants in conversations about democracy, with little use of prompts. All conversations, during each step of this project, were recorded with the permission of informants and transcribed. Notes were also taken after each interview.

9. Nina Eliasoph, *Avoiding Politics: How Americans Produce Apathy in Everyday Life* (Cambridge: Cambridge University Press, 1998), 16.
10. Jane J. Mansbridge, *Beyond Adversary Democracy* (Chicago: University of Chicago Press, 1980).
11. Arlie Russell Hochschild, *Strangers in Their Own Land: Anger and Mourning on the American Right* (New York: New Press, 2016).
12. Katherine J. Cramer, *The Politics of Resentment: Rural Consciousness in Wisconsin and the Rise of Scott Walker* (Chicago: University of Chicago Press, 2016).
13. Francesca Polletta, *Freedom Is an Endless Meeting: Democracy in American Social Movements* (Chicago: University of Chicago Press, 2002).
14. Michael Ignatieff, *The Ordinary Virtues* (Cambridge: Harvard University Press, 2017).
15. For example, and this list is by no means comprehensive, see Hannah Arendt, *Man in Dark Times* (New York: Harcourt Brace, 1970); Zygmunt Bauman, *Liquid Life* (Cambridge, U.K.: Polity, 2005); Ulrich Beck, *Risk Society: Towards a New Modernity* (London: Sage, 1992); Daniel Bell, *The Cultural Contradictions of Capitalism* (New York: Basic Books, 1976); Daniel Bell, "The Social Framework of the Information Society," in *The Microelectronics Revolution*, ed. Tom Forester (Cambridge: MIT Press, 1980), 500–549; Robert N. Bellah, Richard Madsen, William M. Sullivan, Ann Swidler, and Steven M. Tipton, *Habits of the Heart: Individualism and Commitment in American Life* (Berkeley: University of California Press, 1996); Bruce Bimber and Richard Davis, *Campaigning Online: The Internet in U.S. Elections* (Oxford: Oxford University Press, 2003); Jay G. Blumler and Michael Gurevitch, "The New Media and Our Political Communication Discontents: Democratizing Cyberspace," *Information, Communication & Society* 4, no. 1 (2001): 1–13; Pierre Bourdieu and James S. Coleman, *Social Theory for a Changing Society* (Boulder, Colo.: Westview, 1991); Joseph N. Cappella and Kathleen Hall Jamieson, "News Frames, Political Cynicism, and Media Cynicism," *Annals of the American Academy of Political and Social Science* 546, no. 1 (1996): 71–84; Joseph N. Cappella and Kathleen Hall Jamieson, *Spiral of Cynicism: The Press and the Public Good* (New York: Oxford University Press, 1997); James Carey, "The Press, Public Opinion, and Public Discourse," in *Public Opinion and the Communication of Consent*, ed. Theodore L. Glasser and Charles T. Salmon (New York: Guilford, 1995), 373–402; Andrew Chadwick and Philip N. Howard, *Handbook of Internet Politics* (London: Routledge, 2008); Stephen Coleman, "The Lonely Citizen: Indirect Representation in an Age of Net-

works," *Political Communication* 22, no. 2 (2005): 197–214; Peter Dahlgren, "The Internet, Public Spheres, and Political Communication: Dispersion and Deliberation," *Political Communication* 22, no. 2 (2005): 147–162; Kathryn Dean, *Capitalism and Citizenship: The Impossible Partnership* (London: Routledge, 2003); James S. Ettema and D. Charles Whitney, *Audiencemaking: How the Media Create the Audience* (Thousand Oaks, Calif.: Sage, 1994); Anthony Giddens, *The Consequences of Modernity* (Cambridge, U.K.: Polity, 1990); Roderick P. Hart, "Easy Citizenship: Television's Curious Legacy," *Annals of the American Academy of Political and Social Science* 546, no. 1 (1996): 109–119; John Hartley, *Creative Industries* (Oxford, U.K.: Blackwell, 2005); Susan Herbst, *Numbered Voices: How Opinion Polling Has Shaped American Politics* (Chicago: University of Chicago Press, 1995); Ronald Inglehart and Christian Welzel, *Modernization, Cultural Change, and Democracy* (Cambridge: Cambridge University Press, 2005); Peter Kivisto and Thomas Faist, *Citizenship: Discourse, Theory, and Transnational Prospects* (New York: Wiley, 2007); Melvin Kranzberg, "The Information Age: Evolution or Revolution?" in *Information Technologies and Social Transformation*, ed. Bruce R. Guile (Washington, D.C.: National Academy Press, 1985), 35–54; Christopher Lasch, *The Culture of Narcissism* (New York: Norton, 1979); Carolyn Marvin, *When Old Technologies Were New* (New York: Oxford University Press, 1988); Toby Miller, *Cultural Citizenship: Cosmopolitanism, Consumerism, and Television in a Neoliberal Age* (Philadelphia: Temple University Press, 2007); Karen Mossberger, Caroline J. Tolbert, and Ramona S. McNeal, *Digital Citizenship: The Internet, Society, and Participation* (Cambridge: MIT Press, 2007); Mouffe, *On the Political*; Mouffe, *Democratic Paradox*.

16. Philip N. Howard, *The Digital Origins of Dictatorship and Democracy: Information Technology and Political Islam* (New York: Oxford University Press, 2011); Phillip N. Howard and Muzammil M. Hussain, *Democracy's Fourth Wave? Digital Media and the Arab Spring* (New York: Oxford University Press, 2013).

17. Michael Schudson, "Why Conversation Is Not the Soul of Democracy," *Critical Studies in Mass Communication* 14, no. 4 (1997): 297–309.

TWO
Democracy on the Run

1. Thomas More, *Utopia* (1516), in *The Essential Thomas More*, ed. James J. Greene and John P. Dolan, trans. John P. Dolan (New York: New American Library, 1967).
2. More, *Utopia*, 48.
3. More, *Utopia*, 48.
4. Alexis de Tocqueville, *Democracy in America*, trans. Harvey Mansfield and Delba Winthrop (Chicago: University of Chicago Press, 2000).
5. Jean-Jacques Rousseau, 1750, cited in Michael Schudson, *The Good Citizen: A History of American Civic Life* (New York: Free Press, 1998), 365.

6. John Dewey, *The Public and Its Problems* (New York: Holt, 1927), 383; see also Walter Lippmann, *Public Opinion* (New Brunswick, N.J.: Transaction, 1922); Walter Lippmann, *The Phantom Public* (New Brunswick, N.J.: Transaction, 1925).
7. Jeffrey C. Alexander, *Performance and Power* (Cambridge, U.K.: Polity, 2011); Joseph N. Cappella and Kathleen Hall Jamieson, "News Frames, Political Cynicism, and Media Cynicism," *Annals of the American Academy of Political and Social Science* 546 (1996): 71–85; Joseph N. Cappella and Kathleen Hall Jamieson, *Spiral of Cynicism: The Press and the Public Good* (New York: Oxford University Press, 1997); Joshua Meyrowitz, *No Sense of Place: The Impact of Electronic Media on Social Behavior* (New York: Oxford University Press, 1986).
8. Susan Herbst, *Numbered Voices: How Opinion Polling Has Shaped American Politics* (Chicago: University of Chicago Press, 1993); Susan Herbst, Garrett J. O'Keefe, Robert Y. Shapiro, Mark Lindeman, and Carroll J. Glynn, *Public Opinion* (Boulder, Colo.: Westview, 2004).
9. David Karpf, *The MoveOn Effect: The Unexpected Transformation of American Political Advocacy* (New York: Oxford University Press, 2012); David Karpf, *Analytic Activism* (New York: Oxford University Press, 2016); Daniel Kreiss, *Taking Our Country Back: The Crafting of Networked Politics from Howard Dean to Barack Obama* (New York: Oxford University Press, 2012); Kreiss, *Prototype Publics* (New York: Oxford University Press, 2016).
10. Pablo Boczkowski and Zizi Papacharissi, *Trump and the Media* (Cambridge: MIT Press, 2018); James Curran, Natalie Fenton, and Des Freedman, *Misunderstanding the Internet* (London: Routledge, 2012); Zizi Papacharissi, "The Virtual Sphere: The Internet as a Public Sphere," *New Media & Society* 4, no. 1 (2002): 9–27; Zizi Papacharissi, *A Private Sphere: Democracy in a Digital Age* (Cambridge, U.K.: Polity, 2010).
11. Svetlana Boym, *The Future of Nostalgia* (New York: Basic Books, 2001), 354.
12. Hannah Arendt, *The Human Condition*, 2nd ed. (Chicago: University of Chicago Press, 1958).
13. Hannah Arendt, *On Revolution* (New York: Penguin, 1963); Cornelius Castoriadis, *The Imaginary Institution of Society*, trans. Kathleen Blamey (Cambridge: MIT Press, 1987); Cornelius Castoriadis, *Figures of the Thinkable*, trans. Helen Arnold (Stanford, Calif.: Stanford University Press, 2002); Ernesto Laclau, *New Reflections on the Revolution of Our Time* (London: Verso, 1991).
14. Herbert Blumer, *Symbolic Interactionism* (New York: Prentice Hall, 1969); Svetlana Boym, *Another Freedom: The Alternative History of an Idea* (Chicago: University of Chicago Press, 2010); Ernesto Laclau, *On Populist Reason* (London: Verso, 2005); Fred Turner, *The Democratic Surround* (Chicago: University of Chicago, 2013).
15. Nikolai Gogol, *The Complete Tales of Nikolai Gogol*, trans. Constance Garnett (Chicago: University of Chicago Press, 1985), 123.

16. Craig Calhoun, "Introduction: Habermas and the Public Sphere," in *Habermas and the Public Sphere*, ed. Craig Calhoun (Cambridge: MIT Press, 1992), 1–48; Schudson, *Good Citizen.*

17. Stephen Coleman, "The Lonely Citizen: Indirect Representation in an Age of Networks," *Political Communication* 22, no. 2 (2005): 197–214; Jürgen Habermas, *The Divided West* (Malden, Mass.: Polity, 2004); Chantal Mouffe, *The Democratic Paradox* (London: Verso, 2000).

18. Herbst, *Numbered Voices.*

19. James Carey, "The Press, Public Opinion, and Public Discourse," in *Public Opinion and the Communication of Consent*, ed. Theodore L. Glasser and Charles T. Salmon (New York: Guilford, 1995), 373–402; Roderick P. Hart, "Easy Citizenship: Television's Curious Legacy," *Annals of the American Academy of Political and Social Science* 546 (1994): 109–120; Robert Putnam, "The Strange Disappearance of Civic America," *American Prospect* 24, no. 1 (1996): 34–48.

20. Cappella and Jamieson, "News Frames"; Cappella and Jamieson, *Spiral of Cynicism*; James Fallows, "Why Americans Hate the Media," *Atlantic Monthly* 277, no. 2 (February 1996): 45–64; Thomas E. Patterson, *Out of Order: An Incisive and Boldly Original Critique of the News Media's Domination of America's Political Process* (New York: Knopf, 1993); Patterson, "Bad News, Bad Governance," *Annals of the American Academy of Political and Social Science* 546 (1996): 97–108.

21. Zizi Papacharissi, "The Virtual Sphere: The Internet as a Public Sphere," *New Media & Society* 4, no. 1 (2002): 9–27; Papacharissi, *Private Sphere.*

22. Coleman, "Lonely Citizen"; Schudson, *Good Citizen.*

23. Coleman, "Lonely Citizen"; Mouffe, *Democratic Paradox*; Chantal Mouffe, *On the Political* (London: Routledge, 2005).

24. Phillip N. Howard, *New Media Campaigns and the Managed Citizen* (New York: Cambridge University Press, 2006); Lawrence Grossberg, *Under the Cover of Chaos: Trump and the Battle for the American Right* (London: Pluto, 2018); Samuel C. Woolley and Philip N. Howard, *Computational Propaganda: Political Parties, Politicians, and Political Manipulation on Social Media* (New York: Oxford University Press, 2018).

25. Herbst, *Numbered Voices.*

26. Christopher William Anderson, *Apostles of Certainty: Data Journalism and the Politics of Doubt* (New York: Oxford University Press, 2018); Taina Bucher, *If . . . Then: Algorithmic Power and Politics* (New York: Oxford University Press, 2018); David Karpf, *Analytic Activism: Digital Listening and the New Political Strategy* (New York: Oxford University Press, 2016); Daniel Kreiss, *Prototype Politics: Technology-Intensive Campaigning and the Data of Democracy* (New York: Oxford University Press, 2016).

27. Cappella and Jamieson, "News Frames"; Cappella and Jamieson, *Spiral of Cynicism*; Fallows, "Why Americans"; Patterson, *Out of Order*; Patterson, "Bad News."

28. David Buckingham, *The Making of Citizens* (London: Routledge, 2000).

29. Sheldon Wolin, *Fugitive Democracy: And Other Essays* (Princeton, N.J.: Princeton University Press, 2016), 5.
30. Wolin, *Fugitive Democracy*, 31.
31. Wolin, *Fugitive Democracy*, 31.
32. Wolin, *Fugitive Democracy*, 38.
33. Adam Ferguson, *An Essay on the History of Civil Society* (1767; repr., New Brunswick, N.J.: Transaction, 1980); Wolin, *Fugitive Democracy*, 31.
34. Bruce Bimber, *Information and American Democracy* (Cambridge: Cambridge University Press, 2003).
35. Isaiah Berlin, *The Crooked Timber of Humanity: Chapters in the History of Ideas*, ed. Henry Hardy (London: John Murray, 1990), 13.
36. Elizabeth Anderson, *Value in Ethics and Economics* (Cambridge: Harvard University Press, 1995).
37. Elizabeth Anderson, *Private Government: How Employers Rule Our Lives (and Why We Don't Talk About It)* (Princeton, N.J.: Princeton University Press, 2017).
38. Nathan Heller, "The Philosopher Redefining Equality," *New Yorker*, December 31, 2018, https://www.newyorker.com/magazine/2019/01/07/the-philosopher-redefining-equality.
39. Anderson, *Value in Ethics*.
40. Stephan Coleman, *How Voters Feel* (Cambridge: Cambridge University Press, 2013).
41. Boym, *Future of Nostalgia*.

THREE

To Be a Citizen

1. Aristotle (384–322 BC), *The Politics of Aristotle*, trans. Benjamin Jowett (Sioux Falls: NuVision, 2004).
2. Thomas H. Marshall, "Citizenship and Social Class," in *The Welfare State Reader*, 2nd ed., ed. Christopher Pierson and Francis G. Castles (Cambridge, U.K.: Polity, 2006), 30–39.
3. Derek Heater, *A Brief History of Citizenship* (New York: NYU Press, 2004); John Schwarzmantel, *Citizenship and Identity: Towards a New Republic* (London: Routledge, 2003).
4. Zizi Papacharissi, *A Private Sphere: Democracy in a Digital Age* (Cambridge, U.K.: Polity, 2010).
5. Fred Turner asked this question in *The Democratic Surround: Multimedia and American Liberalism from World War II to the Psychedelic Sixties* (Chicago: University of Chicago Press, 2013). I am just repeating his most excellent question.
6. Jean-Jacques Rousseau, 1750, quoted in Michael Schudson, *The Good Citizen: A History of American Civic Life* (New York: Free Press, 1998), 365.
7. Alexis de Tocqueville, *Democracy in America*, trans. Harvey Mansfield and Delba Winthrop (Chicago: University of Chicago Press, 2000).

8. John Dewey, *The Public and Its Problems* (New York: Holt, 1927).

9. Walter Lippmann, *The Phantom Public* (New Brunswick, N.J.: Transaction, 1925).

10. Charles Wright Mills, *White Collar: The American Middle Classes* (New York: Oxford University Press, 1953); Mills, *The Power Elite* (New York: Oxford University Press, 1956).

11. David Riesman, Nathan Glazer, and Reuel Denney, *The Lonely Crowd*, abridged and revised ed. (New Haven: Yale University Press, 2001; orig. pub. 1950).

12. Edward R. Murrow, "Radio Television News Director Address," October 15, 1958, Chicago, Illinois.

13. Kenneth Gergen, *The Saturated Self: Dilemmas of Identity in Contemporary Life* (New York: Basic Books, 1991).

14. Richard Sennett, *The Fall of Public Man* (New York: Norton, 1976).

15. Sennett, *Fall of Public Man*, 20.

16. Hannah Arendt, *Between Past and Future* (New York: Penguin, 1977), 4. I previously discussed this point at greater length in *A Private Sphere*.

17. Safiya Umoja Noble, *Algorithms of Oppression: How Search Engines Reinforce Racism* (New York: NYU Press, 2018).

18. Virginia Eubanks, *Automating Inequality: How High-Tech Tools Profile, Police, and Punish the Poor* (New York: St. Martin's, 2018).

19. Schudson, *Good Citizen*, 311.

20. Schudson, *Good Citizen*, 310.

21. Catherine Knight Steel and Jessica Lu, "Defying Death: Black Joy as Resistance Online," in *A Networked Self and Birth, Life, Death*, ed. Zizi Papacharissi (New York: Routledge, 2019), 143–159; André Brock, *Distributed Blackness: African American Cybercultures* (New York: NYU Press, 2020).

22. Schudson, *Good Citizen*; Lauren Berlant, "Affect, Noise, Silence, Protest: Ambient Citizenship" (paper presented at the International Communication Association Conference, Chicago, May 2009).

23. Hannah Arendt, *The Human Condition*, 2nd ed. (Chicago: University of Chicago Press, 1958); Richard Sennett, *The Craftsman* (New Haven: Yale University Press, 2008).

24. Michael Ignatief, *The Ordinary Virtues* (Cambridge: Harvard University Press, 2017).

25. Marcel Mauss, *The Gift*, trans. W. D. Halls (London: Routledge, 1990); Richard Sennett, *Together* (New Haven: Yale University Press, 2012).

26. I talk about these practices extensively in *Affective Publics: Sentiment, Technology, and Politics* (New York: Oxford University Press, 2015); *Private Sphere*; and *Networked Self*.

27. Jeffrey C. Alexander, *Performance and Power* (Cambridge, U.K.: Polity, 2011).

28. Clifford Geertz, *Negara* (Princeton, N.J.: Princeton University Press, 1980); Erving Goffman, *The Presentation of Self in Everyday Life* (New York: Doubleday, 1959); Goffman, *Behavior in Public Places: Notes on the Social Organization of Gatherings* (New York: Simon and Schuster, 1963); Chantal Mouffe, *The Democratic*

Paradox (London: Verso, 2000); Chantal Mouffe, *On the Political* (London: Routledge, 2005); Victor W. Turner, *Dramas, Fields, and Metaphors: Symbolic Action in Human Society* (Ithaca, N.Y.: Cornell University Press, 1974).

29. Mouffe, *Democratic Paradox.*

30. Stephen Coleman, "The Lonely Citizen: Indirect Representation in an Age of Networks," *Political Communication* 22, no. 2 (2005): 197–214.

31. Mouffe, *Democratic Paradox*, 104, 105.

32. Mouffe, *On the Political*, 52.

33. Mouffe, *On the Political*, 20.

34. Kate Crawford, "Can an Algorithm Be Agonistic? Ten Scenes from Life in Calculated Publics," *Science, Technology, & Human Values* 41, no. 1 (2016): 77–92.

FOUR

Toward the New

1. Hannah Arendt, *On Revolution* (New York: Penguin, 1963).

2. Raymond Williams, *The Long Revolution* (London: Chatto and Windus, 1961).

3. Cornelius Castoriadis, *The Imaginary Institution of Society*, trans. Kathleen Blamey (1987; repr., Cambridge: MIT Press, 1998).

4. Victor Turner, *The Forest of Symbols: Aspects of Ndembu Ritual* (Ithaca, N.Y.: Cornell University Press, 1970); Turner, *Dramas, Fields, and Metaphors: Symbolic Action in Human Society* (Ithaca, N.Y.: Cornell University Press, 1974).

5. Turner, *Forest of Symbols*, 97.

6. Turner, *Dramas, Fields, and Metaphors*, 225.

7. Deen Freelon, Lori Lopez, Meredith D. Clark, and Sarah J. Jackson, "How Black Twitter and Other Social Media Communities Interact with Mainstream News" (Knight Foundation Report, February 27, 2018); Zizi Papacharissi and Meggan T. Trevey, *Affective Publics and Windows of Opportunity: Social Movements and the Potential for Social Change*, ed. Graham Meikle (London: Routledge, 2018), 87–96.

8. Antonio Gramsci, *Selections from the Prison Notebooks of Antonio Gramsci* (New York: International, 1971).

9. Claude Lévi-Strauss, *Introduction to Marcel Mauss* (London: Routledge, 1987), 63–64.

10. Ernesto Laclau, *Emancipation(s)* (London: Verso, 1996).

11. Ernesto Laclau, *On Populist Reason* (London: Verso, 2005).

12. Thomas Patterson, *Out of Order: An Incisive and Boldly Original Critique of the News Media's Domination of America's Political Process* (New York: Knopf, 1993). See also Joseph N. Cappella and Kathleen Hall Jamieson, *Spiral of Cynicism: The Press and the Public Good* (New York: Oxford University Press, 1997).

13. Melvin Kranzberg, "Technology and History: Kranzberg's Laws," *Technology and Culture* 27, no. 3 (1986): 544–560.

14. Eric A. Posner and E. Glen Weyl, *Radical Markets: Uprooting Capitalism and Democracy for a Just Society* (Princeton, N.J.: Princeton University Press, 2018).

FIVE
Before Democracy

1. Andrew Rojecki, *America in the Age of Insecurity* (Baltimore: Johns Hopkins University Press, 2016).

2. Joseph N. Cappella and Kathleen Hall Jamieson, "News Frames, Political Cynicism, and Media Cynicism," *Annals of the American Academy of Political and Social Science* 546, no. 1 (1996): 71–84; Robert M. Entman, "Framing: Toward Clarification of a Fractured Paradigm," *Journal of Communication* 43, no. 4 (1993): 51–58; Richard Grusin, *Premediation: Affect and Mediality After 911* (New York: Palgrave Macmillan, 2010); John Hartley, *Communication, Cultural and Media Studies: The Key Concepts* (London: Routledge, 2012); Daniel Kahneman, *Thinking, Fast and Slow* (New York: Farrar, Straus and Giroux, 2011); Daniel Kahneman and Amos Tversky, *Choices, Values and Frames* (New York: Cambridge University Press, 2000); Sharon Meraz and Zizi Papacharissi, "Networked Gatekeeping and Networked Framing on #egypt," *International Journal of Press/Politics* 18, no. 2 (2013): 138–166; Eric A. Posner and E. Glen Weyl, *Radical Markets: Uprooting Capitalism and Democracy for a Just Society* (Princeton, N.J.: Princeton University Press, 2018); Sue Robinson, "Searching for My Own Unique Place in the Story: A Comparison of Journalistic and Citizen-Produced Coverage of Hurricane Katrina's Anniversary," in *Journalism and Citizenship: New Agendas in Communication*, ed. Zizi Papacharissi (New York: Routledge, 2009), 166–188; Richard Sennett, *The Corrosion of Character: The Personal Consequences of Work in the New Capitalism* (New York: Norton, 1998); Richard Sennett, *Respect in a World of Inequality* (New York: Norton, 2003); Richard Sennett, *The Culture of the New Capitalism* (New Haven: Yale University Press, 2006); Joseph E. Stiglitz, *The Great Divide: Unequal Societies and What We Can Do About Them* (New York: Norton, 2015).

3. See, for example, Posner and Weyl, *Radical Markets*.

4. Mike Ananny, "The Whitespace Press: Designing Meaningful Absences into Networked News," in *Remaking the News*, ed. Pablo J. Boczkowski and C. W. Anderson (Cambridge: MIT Press, 2017), 129–146; Ananny, "Presence of Absence: Exploring the Democratic Significance of Silence," in *Digital Technology and Democratic Theory*, ed. Helene Landemore, Rob Reich, and Lucy Bernholz (Chicago: University of Chicago Press, in press).

5. Stephan Coleman, *How Voters Feel* (Cambridge: Cambridge University Press, 2013).

6. Joshua Meyrowitz, *No Sense of Place: The Impact of Electronic Media on Social Behavior* (New York: Oxford University Press, 1986).

7. I have issued a similar call to "forget messiahs," albeit in more direct and different language, in "Forget Messiahs," *Social Media+ Society* 5, no. 3 (2019): 1–3.

8. Some of this material appeared in an earlier form in Pablo Boczkowski and Zizi Papacharissi, *Trump and the Media* (Cambridge: MIT Press, 2018).

9. Entman, "Framing," 52.

10. See Hartley, *Communication*, 166, for the comprehensive typology of news values.

11. I borrow this phrase from Lisa Gitelman and apply it to the context of news headlines. Gitelman, *Always Already New: Media, History, and the Data of Culture* (Cambridge: MIT Press, 2006).

12. Meraz and Papacharissi, "Networked Gatekeeping."

13. Grusin, *Premediation*.

14. Zizi Papacharissi, *Affective Publics: Sentiment, Technology, and Politics* (New York: Oxford University Press, 2015).

15. For example, the Hutchins Committee in the United States, but also, more informal press coalitions formed around the world when democracy is in crises or in the course of dictatorial regimes.

16. James Hamilton, *Democracy's Detectives* (Cambridge: Harvard University Press, 2016).

17. Frank Pasquale, *The Black Box Society: The Secret Algorithms that Control Money and Information* (Cambridge: Harvard University Press, 2015).

18. Nick Couldry and Ulises A. Mejias, "Data Colonialism: Rethinking Big Data's Relation to the Contemporary Subject," *Television & New Media* 20, no. 4 (2019): 336–349.

19. Mirca Madianou, "Technocolonialism: Digital Innovation and Data Practices in the Humanitarian Response to Refugee Crises," *Social Media+ Society* 5, no. 3 (2019): 1–13.

20. Zizi Papacharissi and Elaine Yuan, "What If the Internet Did Not Speak English? New and Old Language for Studying Newer Media Technologies," in *The Long History of New Media*, ed. David W. Park, Nicholas W. Jankowski, and Steve Jones (New York: Peter Lang, 2011), 89–108.

Index

Index

Campaigns, 88–89, 106, 113. *See also* Elections

Canada, 10, 78, 91, 98

Capitalism, 4, 5; communism and, 21; in conversations, 43; corruption and, 104, 105; democracy and, 42, 43, 89–91, 92; dissatisfaction with, 90; elections and, 89–90; fusion with public geography, 66; influence of, 105–107; shortcomings of markets, 90–92; soft, 90–92, 105, 113, 130, 131

Change, 78–80; agents of, 127–130

China, 11, 33, 98; meaning of citizenship in, 53–54

Choices, 32–33; dissatisfaction with, 109; lack of, 87–88, 102, 106; populist rhetoric and, 82

Citizen: as agent of change, 128–130; craftsman (*homo faber*) model, 71–72; global, 60–61; good, 2; interaction, need for opportunities of, 103; invisible, 63–76, 103; lack of universally accepted model of, 64; meaning of, 7; monitorial, 69–71; noble, 58–63, 67, 102; responsibility of, 45–46, 53, 54, 57; virtuous life and, 52

Citizenship, 13, 51–76, 99, 102–103; civil aspects of, 53, 54, 64, 72; cultural assimilation and, 54–55; difficulty of defining, 51, 58; emergence of, 57–58; equality and, 53, 56; flexibility of concept, 58, 62; in Greco-Roman period, 52; models of, 53; nationality and, 52–53; need for information and, 69–70; performances of, 73; play, fun, satire and, 72–73; political aspects of, 53, 54; social aspects of, 53–56; technology and, 59; themes in, xiii–xiv; virtuous life and, 56

Civic engagement. *See* Community involvement; Voting

Civic literacy, 80, 93–96, 100. *See also* Education

Civility, and politeness, 14

Clinton, Bill, 117

Clinton, Hillary, 122

Cocteau, Jean, 136

Coleman, Stephen, 17, 47

Collectivity, and visibility, 66, 67–68

Colonialism, technological, 133–136

Commercialism, 94. *See also* Capitalism

Communication: commercialism and, 94; by politicians, with electorate, 70, 113; populism and, 84; social media as, 4–5

Communism, and capitalism, 21

Community, 103, 107–108, 126

Community involvement, 70–71, 72, 92. *See also* Micro-governance

Competition, 90

Compromises, 30–31, 73

Connection, 7, 59. *See also* Technology

Consensus, conflictual, 75

Conversations about democracy. *See* Democracy—conversations with informants about

Corporations, 61, 89, 90

Corruption, 1, 11, 60, 86–92, 96, 103, 114; capitalism and, 104, 105; in conversations, 43; effects of, 100; in elections, 89

Countries, 10–12

Covid-19 pandemic, xv

Craftsman (*homo faber*), 71–72

Craftsman, The (Sennett), 2

Cramer, Kathy, 14

Cynicism and disillusionment, 3, 4, 10, 29, 32, 48–49, 99, 102, 107; media

Index

Exclusion, 74
Expression, 4, 7, 12

Facebook, 4, 17, 101, 122, 134
Familiarity, 33–35, 100
Farage, Nigel, 118
Federal system of governance, 108
Ferguson, Adam, 37
Flexibility: of citizenship, 58, 62; of democracy, 42–43, 49
Fraternity, 34
Freedom, 25, 34, 38–40, 43
Freedom Is an Endless Meeting (Polletta), 14
Fugitive democracy, 36, 37
Future, 73, 135, 136

Geography, public, 66
Germany: European Union and, 32; meaning of citizenship in, 52–53, 54–55; transition in, 78
Ghana, 12
Gogol, Nikolai, 27
Good Citizen, The (Schudson), 68
Gorbachev, Mikhail, 33
Governance: absence of experience in, 114; capitalism's influence on, 105–107; in changing and improving democracy, 81; civic republican model of, 56–57; democracy as form of, 37; federal system of, 108; information on, 70; liberal model of, 56–57, 58; micro-governance, 92, 107–108, 113, 130; planning in, 110–111, 113, 130–131; transhuman, 132–137
Gramsci, Antonio, 83
Greece, 10, 44, 98, 118; ancient, 3, 52; and European Union (Grexit referendum), 31, 32, 44, 78; meaning of citizenship in, 56
Grusin, Richard, 121

Habermas, Jürgen, 8
Hamilton, James, 128
Hate speech, technology and, 5, 16
Hegemony, 83
Herbst, Susan, 31
Hochschild, Arlie, 14
How Voters Feel (Coleman), 17

Identity, freedom and, 41
Ignatief, Michael, 15
Imperialism, digital, 133–136
In-between bonds, 67, 71, 92
India, origins of democracy and, 3
Indignados movement, 90, 125
Information, 93, 114; access to, 57, 69, 70; disinformation and misinformation, 6, 25, 93; as economic good, 123; on governance, 70; literacy, 6; media and, 93–95; need for, 25, 69–70; overload, 69–70; skepticism about, 70
Insecurity, 11, 98, 106
Institutions, changing, 77–78
Intensity, 126–127
Internet, 16, 23–24, 132
Interviews with informants. *See* Democracy—conversations with informants about
Invisibility, 65–76
Iran, 12
Isocrates, 135

Johnson, Boris, 118
Journalists and journalism, 120, 127–128, 129. *See also* Media; News
Joy, 71, 72, 76

Kennedy, John F., 45, 116
Knight Steele, Catherine, 70–71
Kranzberg, Melvin, 91

Index

Laclau, Ernesto, 82–83, 84
Language, technology and, 134–135
Law, equality and, 53
Lévi-Strauss, Claude, 83
Liberal model of governance, 56–57, 58
Life, virtuous, 52, 56
Liminality, 79
Lippmann, Walter, 22–23, 62
Literacy: civic, 93–96, 100; digital, 131; information, 6. *See also* Education
Lobbying, 80
Locke, John, 58
The Lonely Crowd (Riesman et al.), 62–63
Lu, Jessica, 71

Majorities, silent, 81
Majority rule, populism and, 85
Male property owners, 3
Mansbridge, Jane, 14
Media, 31; attention economy and, 64–65; campaign process and, 88; in conversations, 93; cynicism and disillusionment toward, 29, 49, 113; democracy, centrality in, 16; distance between politicians and citizens and, 23–24, 118–121, 122–123; illusion of proximity and, 116–117; information and, 93–95; messiahs' use of, 118; modification of behavior through, 115–118; movements and revolutions and, 125; needs of citizens and, 114; news storytelling and journalists, 118–128; pluralism and, 101; public spaces and, 23–24; reorganization of news experience, 121; reproduction of affective narratives and, 126; Trump's use of, 118; trust of, 127; in ways forward, 131. *See also* Social media

Messiahs, 84, 117–118, 125, 126, 128, 131. *See also* Populism
Mexico, 10, 33, 78, 98; meaning of citizenship in, 55–56
Meyrowitz, Joshua, 115, 116
Micro-governance, 92, 107–108, 113, 130. *See also* Community involvement
Mills, Charles Wright, 62
Minority opinions, 73. *See also* Pluralism
Misinformation, 6, 25, 93
Monarchy, 20
Monitorial modality, 69–71
Monopolies, in democracies, 106
Moral conflicts, 40
More, Thomas, 20–21, 22
Mouffe, Chantal, 8, 73, 74, 75, 82–83
Movements, 78; Arab Spring, 4, 7, 98, 125; Black Lives Matter, 78; Indignados, 125; lack of representative equality and, 6; MAGA, 75, 83–84; media and, 125; Occupy, 75, 78, 90, 125; technology and, 16
Murrow, Edward R., 63

Nationality, meaning of citizenship and, 52–53
News, 93; affective, 122, 125–126; headlines and economics of attention, 118–124, 126; online, 120, 132; reorganization of experience of, 121; trust of, 127; Twitter and, 124–125. *See also* Journalists and journalism; Social media
New Yorker, 41
Nixon, Richard, 116
Nobility, of citizen, 58–63, 67, 102
Noise, 32–33, 100
No Sense of Place (Meyrowitz), 115
Nostalgia, 7–8, 24, 29–30, 32, 49